DRIVE THE FOSSE WAY

THE ANCIENT ROMAN ROAD FROM EXETER TO LINCOLN

MICROCAMPER
C A P E R S

DREAM ROADTRIPS AT YOUR FINGERTIPS

ROMAN ROAD SERIES

ROMAN BRITAIN

Britain was a part of the Roman Empire for nearly 400 years. The map of
modern Britain still bears traces of Rome's occupation of the island. The network
of Roman roads still serves as the foundation of our road system in many areas,
such as Ermine Street (the Great North Road/A1) from London to York or
Watling Street (the A5) from London to Wales. Many Roman-era towns, such as
London, York, Canterbury, Exeter, and Carlisle, are still important today.

CONTENTS

FOSSE WAY OVERVIEW MAP

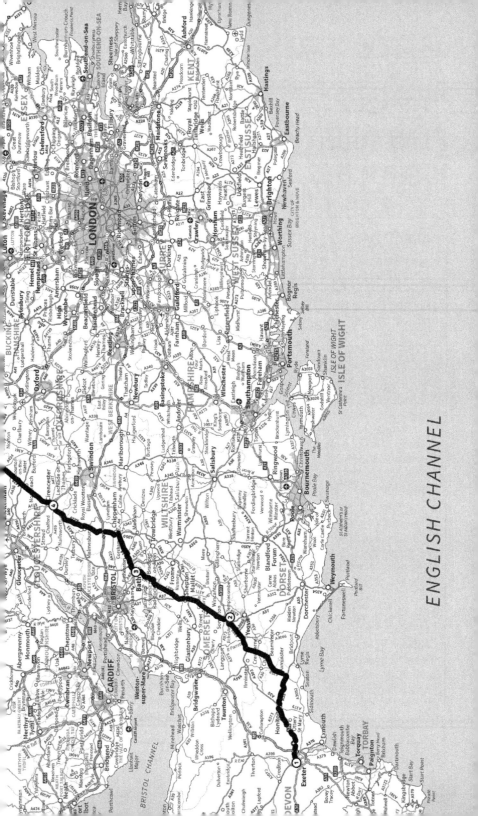

ENGLISH CHANNEL

PLAN YOUR HIGHLIGHTS

Bath

ADVENTURE	ARCHITECTURE	EATS
From exploring medieval tunnels to scampering up castle stairs, there's plenty to conquer.	The buttery-yellow Regency buildings of Bath and picturesque Cotswold villages await you.	Devour a wealth of tasty delights including many well-known, protected-status English nibbles a and a host of tipples.

Exeter's Tunnels

A hidden archaeological wonder lies beneath the hustle and bustle of the High Street with these passages running several metres underground.

Dumpdon Hill Fort

A magnificent Iron Age fort at the top of one of the Otter Valley's most picturesque hills. The challenging ascent is worth the effort, treating you to stunning vistas.

Warwick Castle

Clamber up to the wall walk and take in the stunning views over the river or dive down deep into the dank dungeons.

Pulteney Bridge

Completed in 1774, this shop-lined bridge brings a touch of Italy to Bath, invoking thoughts of Florence's Ponte Vecchio.

Lincoln Cathedral

John Ruskin called this place 'the most precious piece of architecture in the British Isles and roughly speaking worth any two other cathedrals we have'.

Combe Down Tunnel

Opened in 1874, this 1,672 metre long disused railway tunnel was once the UK's longest without intermediate ventilation.

Clotted cream fudge

Originally produced to extend the shelf life of regular cream, the clotted variety soon became embedded in wonderful creamy fudge.

Exeter pudding

Mrs Beeton featured this breadcrumb-based pudding in her book. Laced with rum and jam, and layered with biscuits it is a throwback to Devonian smugglers.

Lincolnshire sausages

With an open, chunky texture, of coarsely ground rather than minced pork they are flavoured with sage. Perfect for breakfast.

The Cotswolds

GARDENS	HISTORY	NATURE
Relax and take some time to hop off the merry-go-round of everyday life.	From the Roman Age to the Space Age, the Fosse Way links some formidable sights.	Stroll through country parks and nature reserves. Visit centres to see wildlife up close.

Kinver Court

Beautifully framed by the sweeping curve of the listed Charlton Viaduct, this garden has appeared on the BBC's Gardeners' World.

Alexandra Park

Perched on the summit of a wooded hill overlooking Bath, this park rewards your uphill slog with stunning vistas of the city.

Lincoln Arboretum

Originally designed and laid out between 1870 and 1872 by Edward Milner, one of the most celebrated Victorian gardeners of his time, enjoy the planting, lakes and bridges.

Roman Baths

Immerse yourself in ancient history and see how Bath's former residents relaxed all those centuries ago, with displays and CGI.

National Space Centre

Discover galleries crammed full of rockets, satellites, and meteorites. Visit the UK's largest planetarium, and ascend the iconic Rocket Tower.

Richard III Centre

Explore the incredible tale of the last English king to die in battle and the first to have his DNA tested, then visit his new resting place in the nearby cathedral.

Cotswold Falconry

Learn about how different species hunt and catch their prey, plus the skill sets that make them successful predators.

Whisby Nature Park

150 hectares of natural habitat, including a complex flooded gravel pits that have been reclaimed by 40 years of natural colonisation.

Wildwood Escot

See red squirrels dart through the trees. Despite their red coats they blend in surprisingly well with their surroundings, so look carefully to spot them.

HOW TO USE THIS GUIDE

1. Choose your start point, Exeter or Lincoln.

2. Browse the stage overview map.

3. Make a list of what you'd like to see. The descriptions of the points of interest broadly follow the sequence of the route.

4. Decide where you're going to break your journey and pick where you're going to camp (either stealth camping or on an official campsite.)

5. Add the stage waypoints and your points of interest to your phone map or sat nav to guide you as your drive.

6. Check your digital route against the paper maps to make sure you stay on the Fosse route (and not the speedy M1. :))

7. Turn up the tunes, hit the road, and enjoy your adventure!

See the full route on Google Maps: **https://rebrand.ly/fw-full**

REMEMBER

Sat navs can take you on inappropriate routes that might not be suitable for your vehicle (or your constitution!) If it's getting tricky, stop and re-plan.

Check the websites for places you plan to visit for opening times, prices and further information to avoid disappointment.

THE FOSSE WAY

Running from Exeter in Devon to Lincoln in the northeast, the Fosse Way is one of Britain's straightest Roman roads.

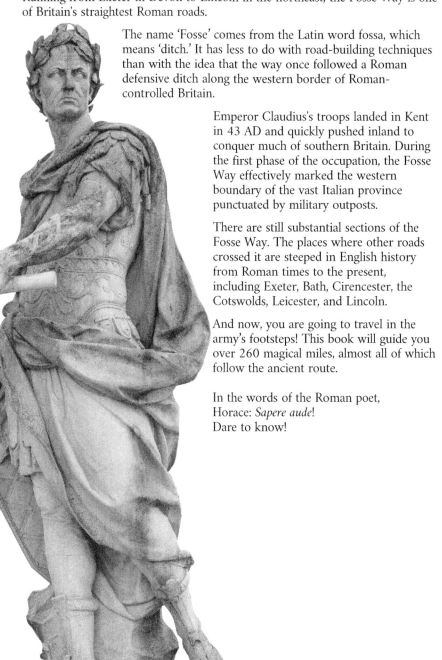

The name 'Fosse' comes from the Latin word fossa, which means 'ditch.' It has less to do with road-building techniques than with the idea that the way once followed a Roman defensive ditch along the western border of Roman-controlled Britain.

Emperor Claudius's troops landed in Kent in 43 AD and quickly pushed inland to conquer much of southern Britain. During the first phase of the occupation, the Fosse Way effectively marked the western boundary of the vast Italian province punctuated by military outposts.

There are still substantial sections of the Fosse Way. The places where other roads crossed it are steeped in English history from Roman times to the present, including Exeter, Bath, Cirencester, the Cotswolds, Leicester, and Lincoln.

And now, you are going to travel in the army's footsteps! This book will guide you over 260 magical miles, almost all of which follow the ancient route.

In the words of the Roman poet, Horace: *Sapere aude!* Dare to know!

THE ROMAN INVASION

Roman re-enactor

When was it?

In 55 BC, Julius Caesar led an expedition to Britain and returned in 54 BC. Both times he defeated the Celts, but he did not stay. Instead, the Celts agreed to pay an annual tribute and the Julius withdrew. In 43 AD, the Romans invaded Britain once more, under Emperor Claudius. The invasion force was made up of 20,000 legionaries and

20,000 auxiliary soldiers from the provinces of the empire, led by Aulus Plautius.

Aulus arrived in Southeast England (the exact location is uncertain) and swiftly defeated the Celtic army, unable to match the discipline and training of the Romans. A battle was fought on the River Medway that resulted in Celtic defeat and rapid withdrawal. The Romans pursued their foes across the Thames into Essex, and within months of their arrival, they had conquered the Celtic hill fort at Colchester.

Meanwhile, other legionaries marched into Sussex, where the friendly Atrebates tribe put up no opposition. The army then marched into Dorset and southern Somerset, the territory of another tribe, the Durotriges.

Victorious, 11 Celtic kings surrendered to Claudius that year, becoming the emperor's loyal puppets. By 47 AD, the Romans controlled England from the Humber River to the Severn Estuary. The war, however, was far from over. The Romans were harassed by the Silures in South Wales and the Ordovices in the North. For years, fighting raged between the Welsh tribes and the imperial force.

Meanwhile, the East Anglian Iceni tribe rebelled. Initially, the Romans allowed them to keep their ruler and have some autonomy. This independence was swiftly removed. The Romans alienated the Iceni in the years that followed by imposing heavy taxes. Then, when the Iceni king died, he left his kingdom to his wife, Boudicca, and to Emperor Nero.

Nero quickly developed a desire for the entire kingdom. His men mistreated the Iceni, stirring up rebellion. The Celtic insurgency was initially successful because a large portion of the Roman army was fighting in Wales at the time. The Celts burned Colchester, St Albans, and London, led by Boudicca.

The Romans dispatched troops to quell the uprising. Despite being outmanned, the Romans were victorious once more because of their superior discipline and tactics. After Boudicca's uprising, the Celts in the southern and eastern regions settled down and gradually accepted Roman rule.

In 71-74 AD, the Romans conquered the north of 'England'. Between 122-126 AD, to keep the Picts out, Emperor Hadrian built a massive wall along the northern border of Roman Britain.

By the middle of the 3rd century, the Roman Empire had fallen into disarray. In the latter half of the century, Saxons from Germany began raiding the east coast of Roman Britain.

The raids were, however, insignificant at first, and most of Roman Britain remained peaceful and prosperous.

In the 4th century, the Roman Empire experienced severe economic and political decline in the west. The population of settlements had shrunk. Amphitheatres and public baths were decommissioned. Scots from Northern Ireland, Picts from Scotland, and Saxons formed an alliance in 367 AD to raid and plunder Roman Britain. The raiding increased after some Roman soldiers were removed in 383.

The last Roman troops began to leave Britain in around 407, according to legend. The Romano-Celt leaders wrote to the Roman Emperor Honorius in 410 AD, pleading for help. Lacking extra forces, the emperor told the Britons that they would have to defend themselves. Despite the division of Roman Britain into kingdoms, they continued to fight Saxon raiders.

Roman civilisation deteriorated over time. People in the towns began bartering instead of using coins. On their estates, the wealthy were left to fend for themselves. Craftsmen relocated to the countryside to eke out a living. Until the mid-fifth century, Roman towns were broadly inhabited. After that, most of them were abandoned. It's possible that farming land both inside and outside the walls may have allowed a small number of people to survive. However, their way of life in settlements came to an end and in the 5th century, Roman civilisation faded away.

ROME'S INFLUENCE

How can scholars learn about such a distant epoch when Roman Britain ended 1,500 years ago? Thankfully, because Britain was a part of Rome's vast empire, some written records have survived, and a handful of Roman historians mentioned Britain when something important needed recording.

Three documentary sources provide the majority of our knowledge of Roman Britain's geography, particularly the Latin names for many forts and towns.

Ptolemy, a Greek geographer working in Egypt's Alexandria in the early 2nd century, gave the location of several named sites as well as many tribes, including those beyond Scotland and Ireland's borders.

The *Antonine Itinerary*, which was written around 100 years later, provides a list of distances between locations on roads used by the imperial messenger service.

The much later 7th century *Ravenna Cosmography* includes a list of names in Britain, but the manuscript is difficult to understand because some names have become distorted and many cannot be located with certainty.

Since at least the 16th century, people have been fascinated by the physical remains of the past and have attempted to understand and explain them. Throughout the 18th and 19th centuries, research was carried out by scholars educated in classical languages and literature. As a result, people naturally attempted to connect the remains discovered with the information in the written sources.

One of the most remarkable archaeological discoveries in recent years came from the Northumberland fort of *Vindolanda*: a large number of thin wooden panels with ink writing on them. Many of these are administrative documents for the unit stationed there, but there's also personal correspondence about *Cataractonium* (Catterick), *Coria* (Corbridge), and *Luguvalium* (Carlisle).

The most important source of information for our understanding of Roman Britain is archaeology in its broadest sense, from survey and excavation to analysis in museums and laboratories. You will have an opportunity to see some of these sites and artefacts on your trip.

Roman Britain's Demise

Britain left the Roman Empire at the beginning of the 5th century AD. In 406, the army in Britain usurped imperial power by proclaiming Constantine III as its own emperor. Constantine led the army across the Rhine to Gaul, where he was defeated and killed in 411. Because of turmoil elsewhere, such as Rome itself being ransacked in 410, the Roman authorities were unable to re-establish control in Britain.

With the breakdown of the central authority and the weakened army, Britain became vulnerable to the threat of hostile peoples from beyond its borders, as well as suffering internal economic and social collapse.

The ways of life for the aristocracy, army and urban population that had characterised Roman Britain fell apart: towns, villas, and forts were abandoned, coins were no longer circulated, and pottery and other Roman objects were no longer manufactured. Elsewhere, the vast majority continued to live their lives as before, earning a living from the land.

The descendants of these farmers would interact with the incoming peoples, such as the Anglo-Saxons and Scots, to lay the groundwork for the nations we now know as the English, Scots, and Welsh.

The Roman Army

The empire maintained a standing army. In the ancient world, this was almost unheard of. The invasion force that invaded Britain in AD 43 was organised using the protocols established by Augustus (31 BC - 14 AD), the first emperor. He established two complementary branches of the service: legions and auxiliaries.

Each legion housed approximately 5,000 people. Legionaries were Roman citizens who served in the Roman army as heavy infantry.

Non-citizen auxiliaries served in units of 500 or 1,000 men, either cavalry, light infantry, or a combination of the two.

As a result, the army had a wide range of troop and unit types that could be used for everything from set-piece battles to border patrol.

In the 2nd century, the British garrison peaked at around 30,000 men, indicating a significant demand for resources to support them.

On a regular basis, Roman soldiers were paid in cash. This accounts for a significant portion of the Roman coins that entered Britain, and a substantial portion of the silver from the province went to supply the mints.

Each man had a daily food ration in the 1st and 2nd centuries, which consisted primarily of grain, but also of meat and vegetables, as well as olive oil and wine. In addition to meat, animals provided important raw materials: leather, bone, and sinew.

Metals, in particularly iron and bronze, were in high demand for armour, weapons, and tools, whereas wood was used for everything from buildings to carts to firewood. In the 1st century, wood and metal were also used to build military bases. Following that, stone, brick, and tile were used, and the extraction of gravel continued apace.

Many resources needed for the empire were raised as a physical form of taxation and frequently had to be transported over long distances (for example, olive oil from southern Spain), affecting the pattern of ports, roads, and storage facilities.

Goods were transported throughout the Roman world, but there were constraints due to land transportation lagging in terms of innovation. The Romans are famous for their roads, but it was significantly cheaper to transport goods by sea rather than river or land. Nonetheless, the transportation method was usually determined by circumstances rather than choice, and all three methods expanded significantly in the 1st and 2nd centuries AD. Although sea transport was the cheapest and fastest, where 1,000 nautical miles could be covered in 9 days, it was also the riskiest method, subject to the whims of weather and threats from pirates. Also, it was limited by the seasons, as the period between November and March (at least) was often regarded as too unpredictable for safe passage.

According to the analysis of over 900 Roman shipwrecks, the most common size of merchant vessel had a capacity for 75 tonnes of goods or 1500 amphorae, but there were larger vessels capable of transporting up to 300 tonnes of goods.

Located off the Spanish-French Mediterranean border, the wreck of the Port Vendres II, dating from around 40 AD, is one interesting example. The cargo included olive oil, sweet wine, fish sauce, fine pottery, glass, and ingots of tin, copper, and lead—supplied by at least 11 different merchants.

During the imperial period, there was extensive state control over trade to ensure supply, as well as a state merchant fleet to transport those goods. These ships replaced the Republic's system of paying subsidies to encourage private shipowners to enter the market. The state taxed the movement of goods between provinces and controlled many local markets, usually held once a week. The establishment of a new market by a large landowner required approval from the Senate or emperor.

Although banking and money-lending remained primarily a local business, there are records of merchants taking out a loan in one port and repaying it in another once the goods were delivered and sold.

There is also plenty of evidence of a free-trade economy beyond the empire's borders, independent of the larger cities and army camps.

Consolidating Power

Consolidation followed conquest campaigns with the construction of a network of longer-term garrisons based on fortresses for legions, and forts for auxiliaries. Because they were often built to control communication routes such as roads and rivers, separate watchtowers were sometimes built to improve surveillance.

In the 1st and 2nd centuries, signal stations were built along major roads, and in the 4th century, along the north-eastern coast. Watchtowers and signal stations were typically made up of a timber or stone tower in a ditched or walled enclosure. Although military installations are dispersed throughout the United Kingdom, not all of the locations would have been occupied at the same time.

Forts in the south and east are typically associated with the early stages of the conquest, before the army resumed its later advance northwards. Many of the forts in the north and west were only occupied for a short period of time. In Wales, where a significant military presence was installed after the difficult wars of conquest in the late 1st century, sites were gradually thinned out, leaving only a handful of forts occupied into the late Roman period.

Almost all the forts in Scotland are related to the short-lived attempts to conquer the country's south and east. Only in what is now northern England was a significant, long-term military garrison present, particularly along Hadrian's Wall and the routes back to the fortresses of Chester and York.

Hadrian's Wall

Hadrian's Wall, which stretches from the Tyne in the east to the Solway in the west, is perhaps the most remarkable of these fortified structures. It was ordered by Hadrian during his visit to Britain in 122 AD, and it was nearly finished by the time he died in 138. The original plan called for a continuous curtain with gates and watchtowers built by the legions but garrisoned by auxiliary forces in the forts along the Roman road (the Stanegate) from nearby

Corbridge to Carlisle. The eastern half was built in stone, from the outset but the western half was originally a turf and timber structure and later replaced with stone.

Because no part of the wall has survived intact, its height and whether it had crenelations and a wall-walk are subject to debate.

Evidence has been found that at every mile there was a guarded gateway known as a milecastle, with two watchtower turrets between each pair. While what remains might seem to be an impenetrable barrier at first glance, the archaeological studies at the milecastle gates demonstrate that the original purpose of the wall was to control movement rather than prevent it. It acted as a provincial border.

Rome still controlled land to the north of the wall, which was guarded by so-called 'outpost' forts. Evidence for these has been found at Bewcastle, Netherby, Birrens, Risingham, and High Rochester. Following the Roman withdrawal Scotland in the 160s, Hadrian's Wall was recommissioned and remained in use until the early 5th century.

There are historical accounts of trouble on the eastern border in the late 2nd century. However, apart from Emperor Septimius Severus's failed attempt to recapture Scotland in AD 208–11, the 3rd century appears to have seen a lengthy spell of calm in Britain. The barracks at many forts were reconstructed with less troop accommodation, indicating a decline in numbers towards late empire levels.

Coastal Defences

Forts were built in the 3rd and 4th centuries to protect the eastern and southern coasts against North Sea raiders and to serve as bases for naval units. They show clear developments in military design. This is referred to as the 'Saxon Shore' system.

The earliest forts, such as Brancaster on the North Norfolk coast and Reculver on the northern shores of Kent, were built to protect major waterways—sea passages and river estuaries.

The change to the late type can be seen in the Midlands at Bradwell and Norfolk's Burgh Castle, as well as Portchester and Richborough in the south. These forts were square and high-walled. There were small gateways, and regularly spaced outward-looking artillery towers.

This new style of fort was built to be defensible in a way that earlier forts were not, though the internal buildings appear to be much smaller and less organised than those at Hadrian's Wall.

Similar forts on the west coast at Cardiff and Lancaster indicate a threat from across the Irish sea Later in the 4th century. A series of signal stations were built on the north-east coast, most likely to protect against seaborne raiders from north of Hadrian's Wall.

According to historical sources, Britain was raided and attacked throughout the 4th century, with a major setback in AD 367 when hostile peoples combined in a simultaneous attack that overwhelmed both Hadrian's Wall and the 'Saxon Shore', forcing the emperor to send an expeditionary force to restore order. The local Roman military leader, Nectaridus, Count of the Saxon Shore, was killed. A small field army may have been stationed in Britain at this time, though where it was stationed is unknown.

Roman Religion

In the ancient world, religion governed every aspect of life. It explained how the world was created, how nature operated, and where humans came from. It shed light on how people should organise themselves, and how they should act in front of the gods and their fellow citizens. Finally, it provided an answer to the question of what would happen to them after death.

The Roman empire worshipped a diverse range of deities. An individual was not required to worship a single god or goddess. A person could choose which deity to address as appropriate. Sometimes that might be to a local deity to address a local matter, or it could be to a god or goddess who had a beneficial special power, else prayers could be offered to one the worshipper personally favoured. Only Jews and, later, Christians, stood up to system by worshipping one god and declaring that all others were false.

There is evidence for a diverse range of deities in Roman Britain and the worship of living and dead emperors, the imperial family, Roman gods, and Rome itself. This phenomenon arose in part to try to ensure the loyalty of a vast and diverse empire by focusing on the core deities and the imperial family. Most of the evidence for these religious observances in Britain comes from military areas, demonstrating the measures taken to ensure the army's loyalty. The army also provided most of the devotees for the eastern 'mystery cults, which were centred on divine figures such as Mithras (from Persia) or Orpheus (from Greece) who had overcome death and offered their fans the chance to do the same. There is a temple to Mithras in Leicester, and another good example in London.

Local divinities, many of whom predated the conquest, were by far the most numerous in Britain during the Roman period. Some of these were most likely deities of natural features such as springs, rivers, and lakes, while others could have been regional gods or goddesses.

Much like ancient Greek gods, the names of native British deities were sometimes paired with those of the Roman, implying that the two had something in common. An examples of this would be the native god Camulos who was frequently paired with Mars, the god of war, although slower to anger than his Roman counterpart. Modern day Colchester, previously the Roman stronghold of Camulodunum, means 'The Stronghold of Camolus.'

In Britain, only a few temples were built in the classical Greco-Roman style. The Temple of the Deified Claudius in Colchester, Essex, was the largest and most elaborate of this type, serving as the focus of the state religion for the civilian parts of Britain. More of the much smaller temple of Sulis Minerva, who presided over the hot springs in Bath, Somerset, has survived.

The most common type of temple was what is now known as a Romano-Celtic temple. It's difficult to imagine what happened at these temples. They were far too small for congregational worship and could only have been used by priests or individual worshippers. Large crowds may have gathered around the temple or in its precincts during major festivals. Some temple sites have evidence of altars, implying offerings or sacrifice; a few have pits containing deity-related objects. However, the activities that took place at these temples have left as little trace as the beliefs of the people who used them.

Temples were sometimes built on natural features such as hilltops and springs, implying that these places were holy or were the homes of gods. Unlike classical and Romano-Celtic temples, shrines built for devotees of 'mystery' cults were intended to enclose the worshippers and conceal them and their rites from those who had not been initiated into the cult.

Christianity, the last and most successful of the 'mystery' religions, took root in Britain during the late Roman period. Following the persecutions of the 3rd century, the conversion of Emperor Constantine I (306-37 AD) saw Christianity become the empire's dominant religion. Delegations from Britain's four provinces, three of which were led by bishops, attended the Council of Arles in southern Gaul in 314 AD. A few churches with baptisteries have been discovered in towns such as Silchester, Hampshire, Icklingham, Suffolk, and the Saxon Shore fort at Richborough, Kent. The general perception is that Christianity was associated with the upper classes and urban areas. The extent to which it spread among the lower classes and rural populations is unknown.

Roman Burials

Most of the dead were cremated in the first two centuries, and their ashes were frequently accompanied by pottery vessels and other grave goods. From the late 2nd century onward, there was a shift away from cremation towards burial, and the provision of grave goods became less common.

The largest cemeteries were located outside the city limits to avoid contaminating the living with diseases caused by contact with the dead. Many of these burials took place in simple graves with no trace of a marker.

Some, on the other hand, were marked by a tombstone with the deceased's name and age. There was the occasional more elaborate monument. Expensive burials emphasised the importance of their owners at some villas; these included large earthen barrows or mausolea, sometimes in the form of a temple.

Archaeological Finds

Hundreds of coin hoards were buried during the Roman period, in addition to coins deposited at springs, and those buried alongside precious objects such as jewellery and silver plate, as well as other pewter, bronze, and iron metalware. Plate finds are most common near the end of the Roman period, particularly in East Anglia, which may be a testament to the uncertainty of the times but also evidence for entrusting valuables to the protection of the earth's gods. Thousands of coins and a fascinating series of curse tablets calling down vengeance (preferably protracted and painful) on thieves were thrown into the sacred spring at Bath by worshippers.

Sometimes, precious items were buried due to military insecurity, but more often than not, monetary instability. The evidence from temple sites suggests that they could also be regarded as offerings to the gods. The major hoard of early Christian silver plate at Water Newton, Cambridgeshire, and another at Traprain Law, East Lothian, strongly suggest the presence of a Christian community nearby.

Mosaics and wall paintings in villas such as Hinton St Mary, Dorset, and Lullingstone, Kent, indicate that they may have been places of Christian worship.

Roman amphora

STAGE 1

EXETER TO ILCHESTER

55 Miles

Explore wonderful city of Exeter before taking in the rolling Devonshire countryside and into Somerset.

THE ROUTE

EXETER TO LINCOLN

↳	0m	Exeter
↳	17m	Honiton (A30)
↳	10m	Axminster (A35)
↳	12m	Street (A358/B3167)
↳	3m	Chillington
↳	2m	Dinnington Docks
↳	10m	Ilchester (A303)

LINCOLN TO EXETER

↳	0m	Ilchester
↳	10m	Dinnington Docks (A303)
↳	2m	Chillington
↳	3m	Street (A358/B3167)
↳	12m	Axminster (A358)
↳	10m	Honiton (A35)
↳	17m	Exeter (A30)

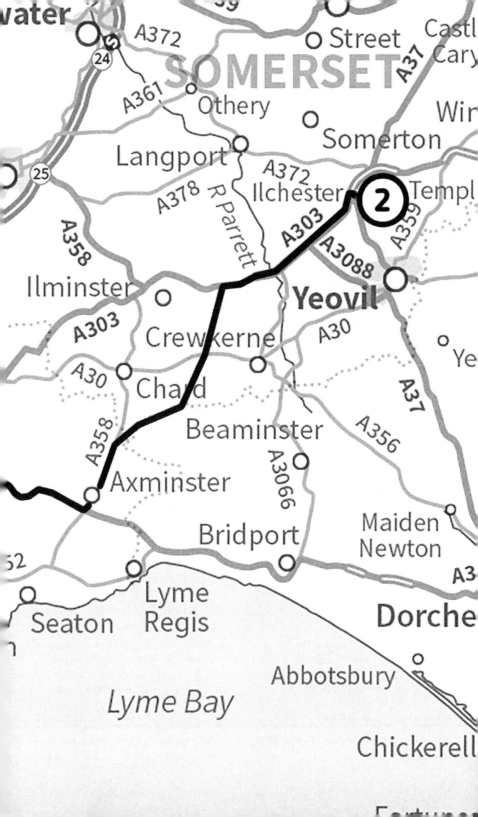

Exeter Cathedral at dusk

Exeter

ISCA DUMNONIORUM

The Romans arrived in the Southwest around 50 AD. They constructed a wooden fort on a hill near the river Exe at its lowest point, where it could be easily crossed. A town was built. The Romans called it Isca.

Like all Roman towns, it had a central rectangular space known as the forum. This had a marketplace, shops, and the basilica, which served as a sort of town hall.

Germanic Saxons invaded the East and reached Devon by the 7th. century They built a monastery inside the old Roman wall in 680.

In 1068. The Normans attempted to capture Exeter for 18 days, but failed. Exeter was finally subdued by William the Conqueror. He built a castle to keep the townspeople in line in future.

Wool making and tanning were the main industries. Exeter used its nearby port to export wool and import fine wines. Butchers, bakers, brewers, carpenters, blacksmiths, and shoemakers were found in the town, too. Skilled workers lived and worked in the same neighbourhood.

Many street names still bear witness to the Exeter hayfields, including Princesshay, Friernhay, Bonhay Road, and the Friern (Friar's) Hay.

Henry VIII closed the priory and the friaries in 1538. This in turn sparked a civil war in 1549. After besieging the city, the rebels were forced to retreat when the royal army arrived.

The English Civil War began in 1642. Exeter initially supported parliament. In June of 1643, the Cornish Royalist Army besieged the town. Exeter had to surrender by the end of September. The city was one of the final Royalist cities

to fall into Parliamentarian hands towards the end of the war.

For the wealthy, life in 18th century Exeter improved. The first newspaper appeared in 1707. The first bank was established in 1769. In the same year, the lavish Assembly Rooms were constructed.

Lamps lighting the streets and pavements for the public had been installed by 1778. Devon and Exeter hospital was built. A new Exe Bridge was constructed, with Bridge Street laid out to get to it.

In 1801, the city was home to 20,000 residents, a settlement city for that time. However, the cities in the Midlands and Northern England surpassed it. The industrial revolution overlooked Exeter.

A cholera epidemic took the lives of 440 people in 1832. Sewers were subsequently built afterward.

Although its population had a small increase, its businesses were struggling. Exeter was sixth-largest city in England in the 1700s.

By 1860, it had fallen to 60th place. Exeter was settling into the role of a quiet market town. Wool manufacture and tanning declined as it became a modest manufacturing centre.

St. Michael's church was built in 1868. Horse-drawn trams ran in the streets from 1882. In 1905, Exeter's horse-drawn trams were replaced by electric ones. Buses became commonplace. The population grew to about 60,000 by 1914. Exeter Airport was opened in 1937.

The city was the victim of a Luftwaffe revenge attack on historic British towns in May 1942 in revenge for the RAF attacks on the historic German towns of Rostock and Lubeck earlier in the year.

In the 1950s, the city centre was rebuilt. Today, the majority of Exeter's workforce is employed in service industries such as tourism, education, and civil projects.

Cathedral statue of St George

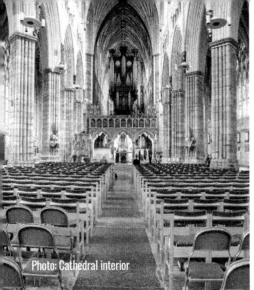
Photo: Cathedral interior

Exeter Cathedral

The Cloisters, Exeter EX1 1HS
www.exeter-cathedral.org.uk

Exeter Cathedral is an Anglican cathedral and the seat of the Bishop of Exeter. It is officially known as the Cathedral Church of Saint Peter in Exeter. The current structure, which was completed around 1400, includes an early set of misericords, an astronomical clock, and the world's longest medieval stone vaulted ceiling.

It was founded in 1050, when the Bishop of Devon and Cornwall's seat was relocated from Crediton due to fears of attack.

The appointment of William Warelwast in 1107 prompted the construction of a new Norman-style cathedral. It was officially begun in 1133, but it took many years to complete. It was constructed entirely of local stone, including Purbeck marble.

Exeter, like most English cathedrals, suffered during the dissolution of the monasteries, but not as much as it would have if it had been a monastic foundation. The cloisters were destroyed during the English Civil War, causing further damage.

During the Victorian era, gothic revival architect Sir George Gilbert Scott renovated the building.

In May 1942, a large Luftwaffe bomb landed directly on the St James Chapel, destroying it. Thankfully, many of the cathedral's most important artefacts, including the ancient glass (including the great east window), the misericords, the bishop's throne, the Exeter Book, the ancient charters (of King Athelstan and Edward the Confessor), and other valuable library documents, had been removed in preparation for an attack. The explosion also obliterated the room above, three aisle bays, and two flying buttresses. The blast shattered the medieval screen opposite the chapel, but it has since been restored.

Following repairs and clearing of the area around the western end, remnants of earlier structures, such as the remains of the Roman city and the original Norman cathedral, were discovered.

Exeter Guildhall

203 High St, Exeter EX4 3EB
www.exeter.gov.uk

The guildhall has been graded I since 1953, and is a listed ancient monument. It was established on the site in 1000 AD, the secular equivalent to the cathedral in terms of influence over the town. It has served as a prison, a courthouse, a police station, a city hall, a record store, a wool market, and as the local meeting

Exeter Guildhall | Neil Owen | Wiki Commons

hall for the City Chamber and Council.

Like many ancient buildings, the guildhall has gone through 'makeovers' throughout the ages, and as a result it contains a range of architectural styles.

The estimated construction date is 1466. Tree-ring dating, gives a range between 1463 and 1498.

Later, the front of the guildhall was pulled down and rebuilt in 1591. Like the modern era, ordinary Elizabethans were expected contribute to city council building projects, which caused much consternation in the community. The building's distinctive pillars and arched entrance are the result of this work. Panelling from the portico's addition in 1594 surrounds the main hall.

This hall was often used for Assizes Courts and Quarter Sessions. Judge Jeffreys, after Monmouth's 1685 rebellion, presided over the 'Bloody

Assizes' at the guildhall. In the main hall, criminals were sentenced to transport, prison, and the gallows. The guildhall's cells have been unused since 1887, though remanded prisoners have been held in them in more recent times.

Horatio Nelson received the freedom of the city in the guildhall in 1801. One of the walls contains a statue of Queen Victoria, commemorating her Golden Jubilee in 1887.

Underground Passages

2 Paris St, Exeter, EX1 1GA
exeter.gov.uk/passages

What remains of a network of medieval tunnels built to supply the city with fresh water can be found beneath the city streets. Falling into disrepair, they were all but been forgotten until they reopened as a tourist attraction in the 20th century. Nowadays, a hidden archaeological wonder lies beneath the hustle and bustle of the High Street. The passages, running for 425 metres through the city centre, lie four and six metres beneath the surface. They have a fascinating tale to tell.

Built in the Middle Ages to house lead pipes that supplied fresh water, the pipes transported water from natural field springs located outside Exeter's city limits. This engineering project required a great deal of planning. To aid maintenance, a system of vaulted tunnels and several entry points was devised.

The first passage was built in 1346 to bring water to Exeter Cathedral in particular. Fresh water became a luxury enjoyed primarily by the clergy because the city was very much an ecclesiastical power at the time. In 1492, the city passage was built, eventually bringing water to Exeter's residents. Only a few of the wealthy had water piped directly to their homes, while most of the population relied on the 'Great Conduit' fountain which brought a communal water supply to street level.

During the Civil War, a section of the passages were blocked off and filled in, due to concerns that opposing forces could use the tunnels to gain access to the city. Following the war's conclusion, they were reopened.

In the 19th century, a widespread outbreak of cholera raised health concerns, prompting the water system to be redesigned in 1832. The old lead pipes were replaced with cast iron pipes, and the passages were levelled to improve water flow and reduce the build-up of stagnant, disease-carrying water. The water source was also relocated to Pynes Hill, where it was treated in a purpose-built facility.

Following a period of inactivity, interest in the underground passages was reignited in the 1930s with guided visitor tours.

Princesshay Shopping

9 Catherine Street, Exeter EX1 1QA
www.princesshay.com

The original Princesshay, which opened in the 1950s, was the country's first pedestrianised shopping street. Before construction began, Princess Elizabeth, after whom the development was named, unveiled a plaque at the site on October 21, 1949. In 2005, archaeological work was undertaken. Over a tonne of Roman tile fragments, rare early 5th century pottery, and 144 coins, one of

Belmont Park

which was minted in the city, were among the discoveries.

The post-war structures were replaced and a new shopping centre was unveiled in September 2007.

Belmont Park

Belmont Rd, Exeter EX4 6SS
https//:www.exeter.gov.uk/parks

One of the city's most popular parks, between Blackboy Road and Belmont Road, this park was one of Exeter's first late-Victorian parks to open its 5-acre doors in 1886. It hosted a pageant of 'Olde Englishe Sportes' the following year to commemorate Queen Victoria's Diamond Jubilee. Later egg and spoon, sack, and wheelbarrow races were all held there during Edward VII's coronation celebrations in 1902. Before the First World War, tourists were encouraged to visit the park to appreciate its diverse plants and trees. In 1939, the

Red squirrels live at Escot

first garden in England designed for the blind was planted. The Belmont Scent Garden, located in the park's east end, contains many of the country's best fragrant plants.

Wildwood Escot

Ottery St Mary, Devon EX11 1LU
devon.wildwoodtrust.org

There is something for everyone here. Amazing animals, a magnificent maze, outdoor adventure play, indoor soft play, terrific traversing walls, heart-stopping drop-slide, a 40 metre zip line, and authentic Saxon village!

Hembury Fort

Payhembury, Honiton, Devon EX14 3LA
www.hemburyfort.co.uk

Hembury is a Neolithic enclosure and Iron Age hill fort near Honiton. It is located at the end of a 240m high ridge in the Blackdown Hills on a south facing promontory. It is located

to the north of, and overlooks, the River Otter valley. This location was most likely chosen for both defensive and aesthetic reasons.

Ottery St Mary

Ottery St Mary, the birthplace of poet Samuel Taylor Coleridge, is about 10 miles east of Exeter. The town square is home to pubs, restaurants, and coffee and tea shops. Stretch your legs, with a walk along the River Otter to see the Tumbling Weir, a swirling whirlpool that looks like a giant plug hole. Admire the imposing church that towers over the town, then meander through the narrow streets lined with more shops, cafés, and restaurants.

Ottery St Mary's circular weir walk

Honiton High Street

Honiton

Although the town grew along the Fosse Way, it's unlikely that the Romans used it as a rest stop because they built a small fort to the west of the current town.

Later, Honiton became a major market town, famous for lace-making, which was introduced by Flemish immigrants in the 1500s. Hundreds of women made lace in their homes in the 17th century, and Queen Victoria had her wedding gown made of Honiton lace. It was also well-known for its pottery production.

Fires in 1747 and 1765 left the town devastated.

The town's Museum of Lace and Local Antiquities claims to have one of the world's most extensive collections of Honiton lace.

It is housed in a building that was once part of Allhallows School and dates to the early 16th century.

The Glen

Honiton, EX14 2GX
www.devongardenstrust.org.uk

The Glen is a 6-acre public woodland park that connects the open countryside to the heart of Honiton. It is in a valley where the Glen stream flows into the Gissage River. A local man, Major H Lilley presented the Lower Glen to the people of Honiton to commemorate King George V's Silver Jubilee in 1935. To mark the occasion, local schoolchildren planted trees, some of which still stand today. It has since been extended to include the Higher Glen and the Millenium Green.

Blackbury Camp [EH]

Southleigh, Colyton, Devon, EX24 6JE
www.english-heritage.org.uk

Built in the 4th century BC, the camp had impressive ramparts. The single entrance was protected by a large triangular earthwork or 'barbican'. Now surrounded by woodland, this hillfort is a popular spot for picnics, although parts of it are uneven and can become muddy. There is a small car park. Note: overnight parking or camping is not currently permitted.

Dumpdon Hill Fort [NT]

Luppitt, Honiton, Devon EX14 4TY
www.nationaltrust.org.uk

Dumpdon is a magnificent Iron Age hill fort that lies at the top of one of the Otter Valley's largest and most picturesque hills. The ascent to the fort is well worth the effort, and the vistas of the surrounding area are stunning. Before investigating the intriguing beech forest, stop to explore the impressive earthworks.

Loughwood Meeting House [NT]

Dalwood, Axminster, Devon EX13 7DU
www.nationaltrust.org.uk

Owned by the National Trust since 1969, Dalwood's historic Baptist chapel is located one mile south of the village. There was a meeting house on this site prior to the late 17th or early 18th century. It is one of the oldest Baptist churches still standing. Except for the surrounding graves, it appeared to be a peasant's home. Constructed of stone rubble, it has buttresses and a thatched roof. The interior was built between the mid-eighteenth and early-nineteenth centuries. In the southwest corner was a stable for the horses of those who travelled long distances. The church had been in existence for some time prior to 1653. Several of the founding members had served in the Parliamentary forces under General Fairfax during the English Civil War.

Axe Valley Wildlife Park

Summerleaze Farm, Kilmington, Devon EX13 7RA
www.axevalleypark.co.uk

A small zoo situated in the beautiful countryside of the Axe Valley in East Devon, just off the A35, primarily aimed at families with children under 12 years of age.

Millers Farm Shop

Gammons Hill, Kilmington, EX13 7RA
www.millersfarmshop.co.uk

This shop has been growing and selling locally sourced produce for over forty years. Perhaps you might pick up something to cook back at the van?

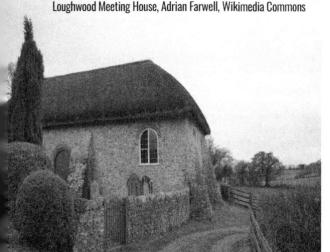
Loughwood Meeting House, Adrian Farwell, Wikimedia Commons

Georgian houses in Axminster

Axminster

Axminster, a lovely market town on the River Axe in the East Devon Area of Outstanding Natural Beauty, is full of traditional charm and character. It was founded around 300 BC during the Celtic period, and is located on two major Roman roads. (Some people argue the Fosse ends at Axminster, but that would mean you'd miss out on Exeter so it made the cut.) The town's history is inextricably linked to the carpet industry, which was founded in 1755 by Thomas Whitty at Court House. Because the early hand-tufted carpets took so much time and effort to complete, they were celebrated with a peal of bells from the nearby parish church. Axminster carpets are still used in Buckingham Palace, Windsor Castle, and other royal residences today.

The town was granted a charter in 1210 that included the right to hold a weekly cattle market, which was held in the market square until 1834, when it was moved to Trinity Square. It was then relocated in October 1912 to a location off South Street, where it remained for the next 94 years.

The town was on the London-to-Exeter coach route. In its heyday, over 16 coaches a day would stop at the hotel for refreshments and horse changes. Axminster was on the Trafalgar Way, the historic route used to transport dispatches with news of the Battle of Trafalgar overland from Falmouth, Cornwall, to the Admiralty in London in 1805. There is a plaque marking this in the town centre.

Hugh Fearnley-Whittingstall, the celebrity chef and TV presenter, has his River Cottage H.Q. farm in the Axe valley. Since then, he's bought an old inn that used to be the town's ballroom and has converted it into an organic produce shop and canteen. The Minster, which stands in a green oasis in the heart of town, was once so prestigious that Saxon princes were buried there.

Axminster Heritage Centre

Silver Street, Axminster EX13 5AH
axminsterheritage.org

This is where you can learn more about the town's carpet industry. Travel back in time to discover what has made Axminster and the surrounding area what they are today. Explore its Bronze and Stone Age origins to its role as a crossroads on the Roman Fosse Way. Learn about the Cistercian monks who built the abbey at Newenham after receiving the Manor of Axminster in 1246. Discover how, over time, Axminster grew into a bustling agricultural market town with a thriving rural economy.

Cricket St Thomas

Cricket House was filmed as the fictitious 'Grantleigh Manor' in the British sitcom television series 'To the Manor Born', broadcast from 1979 to 1981.

Cricket House

River Axe

The River Axe flows through Dorset, Somerset, and Devon. It begins in Dorset near Beaminster and flows west. It then flows south through Axminster, joining the English Channel at Axmouth. Fish include

The Axe at Axmouth

brown trout, dace, roach, and occasional salmon. Much of the river is designated as a site of special scientific interest, and it is home to a diverse array of aquatic life. The river boasts resident otters to look out for.

Perry's Cider Mills

Dowlish Wake, Ilminster, TA19 0NY
www.perryscider.co.uk/open-cidery

Soak in the atmosphere of a real working mill where you can grab a cider or a bite to eat. There is also a small museum on-site, which is housed in the original 16th century thatched cider barn where the company began.

Forde Abbey

Chard, Somerset, TA20 4LU
www.fordeabbey.co.uk

The abbey has a 900-year history and was home to the stunning Mortlake tapestries, which were woven from internationally famous Raphael cartoons and are now housed in the V&A museum London. It has hosted Cistercian monks at prayer, 19th century philosophers, and politicians, been implicated in the Monmouth Rebellion, and most recently, served as the setting for the Hollywood adaptation of Thomas Hardy's 'Far from the Madding Crowd.'

Barrington Court [NT]

Barrington, Somerset, TA19 0NQ
www.nationaltrust.org.uk

An atmospheric piece of old Somerset: an empty Tudor manor house that was beautifully restored in the 1920s, complete with a farm, bountiful flowers, and orchards. NOTE: The sat nav points to the rear of the building. As you approach, follow the brown signs instead.

Dinnington

There is evidence of a Roman villa nearby, which was excavated by the archaeological TV show 'Time Team' in 2002 and 2006. Surface finds of tesserae, roofing slates, and pottery have been made. Coins, as well as a small bronze dog, were also discovered.

Montacute House [NT]

Montacute TA15 6XP
www.nationaltrust.org.uk

Montacute is a treasure trove of Elizabethan Renaissance architecture and design. It is a place of beauty and wonder, with its towering glass walls, golden stone, and surrounding garden and parkland.

Yeovil

Yeovil is located on the main Roman road that connects Dorchester to the Fosse Way at Ilchester. A small Roman town can be found at the Westland site. There were several Roman villas (estates) in the vicinity. East Coker,

Forde Abbey

Montacute House

West Coker, and Lufton have all yielded discoveries. In the Middle Ages, Yeovil was first mentioned as Gifle in an 880 Saxon charter. It is derived from the Celtic river name 'gifl', which means 'forked river,' and was an earlier name for the River Yeo. Explore the town and the nearby Ninesprings Country Park.

Ham Hill

Ham Hill Rd, Stoke-sub-Hamdon, Somerset TA14 6RW
southsomerset.gov.uk

This fort dates from the Iron Age. It is one of the largest in Britain, covering an area of 210 acres. It was also occupied during the Mesolithic and Neolithic eras, as well as the Roman and Medieval. The fort is a Scheduled Ancient Monument, and the entire hill is a geological Site of Special Scientific Interest, as well as a country park.

Tintinhull Garden [NT]

Farm Street, Tintinhull, Somerset BA22 8PZ
www.nationaltrust.org.uk

The garden, which includes a working kitchen garden and an orchard. Shimmering pools, secluded lawns, colourful borders, and neatly clipped hedges provide the ideal setting for relaxation away from the hustle and bustle.

Tintinhull Gardens

Ilchester's historic houses

Ilchester

LINDINIS

AD 60, a timber-walled fort was established at Ilchester, and a second fort appears to have been built later. It guarded the Fosse Way's crossing of the River Yeo.

Originally surrounded by native round houses, it was later replaced by a 30-acre settlement. After the post was abandoned in the late 1st century, a street grid formed with dwellings and workshops, as well as industrial suburbs.

There is evidence of iron, glass, and bone works, as well as pottery production and agricultural plots. The central area was surrounded by a defensive bank and ditch with stone gateways in the late 2nd century.

Stone walls were built in the mid-fourth century. Other than Durnovaria (Dorchester), it became the only walled town in the Durotrige tribes' territory.

The town appears to have largely consisted of luxury private homes owned by rich individuals wealthy enough to instal fine mosaic floors.

More than 30 have been discovered, and it has been suggested that the town housed a workshop of mosaicists from the Corinium Saltire School, or that it had its own 'Lindinis School.'

STAGE 2

ILCHESTER TO BATH

36 Miles

Glide through the Mendips and onto the historic city of Bath, known to the Romans as Aqua Sulis.

THE ROUTE

EXETER TO LINCOLN

- ↳ 0m Ilchester
- ↳ 7m Lydford-on-Fosse (A37)
- ↳ 4m Wraxall (A37)
- ↳ 6m Shepton Mallet (A37)
- ↳ 6m Stratton on the Fosse (A367)
- ↳ 4m Radstock (A637)
- ↳ 9m Bath (A367)

LINCOLN TO EXETER

- ↳ 0m Bath (A367)
- ↳ 9m Radstock (A367)
- ↳ 4m Stratton on the Fosse (A367)
- ↳ 6m Shepton Mallet (A37)
- ↳ 6m Wraxall (A37)
- ↳ 4m Lydford-on-Fosse (A37)
- ↳ 7m Ilchester

Avonmouth
Portishead
A369
M32
M4
A46
BRISTOL
CITY OF BRISTOL
Nailsea
N SOMERSET
Batheaston
A431
Keynsham
A4
A38
A370
A37
Bath
3
Banwell
A368
BATH AND NE SOMERSET
A39
A367
Bradford-on-Avon
Blagdon
Radstock
Cheddar
A366
A36
A38
A371
A362
Frome
Nunney
Wells
Glastonbury
A361
Shepton Mallet
R Frome
A371
A359
Street
Castle Cary
SOMERSET
Bruton
Othery
Wincanton
Somerton
A303
A372
Ilchester
A378
R Parrett
2
Templecombe
A357
A30
A3088
Stalbridge
Yeovil
Sherborne
A3030
Crewkerne
Yetminster
A37

17

Lyneham

Chippenham

A310

A4361

SWINDON

A346

Lamb

W

A4

Calne

Avebury

Marlborough

A350

A342

A4

Hung

Melksham

Devizes

A342

A346

A338

Burbage

A361

Pewsey

owbridge

A342

Ludgersha

Upavon

A342

WILTSHIRE

A345

A338

Westbury

A360

Tilshead

Tidworth

Warminster

Salisbury Plain

A36

Shrewton

A303

A303

Amesbury

Grateley

A34

A338

A30

Wilton

R

Stockbridg

Salisbury

A30

A27

haftesbury

A338

A36

Romsey

A354

Sixpenny
Handley

Downton

M271

rrent
nton

M27

Fordingbridge

R Avon

1

2

Verwood

Lyndhurst

Tott

A31

R
Wim

It is Europe's largest naval aviation museum, with four exhibition halls, over 90 aircraft, over 2 million records, and 30 thousand artefacts. It also houses the world's first British Concorde, which you can board, view the cockpit, and visit the award-winning Aircraft Carrier Experience. There is a café on site.

Motor Museum

Sparkford, Yeovil BA22 7LH
www.haynesmotormuseum.com

John Haynes' love of automobiles and business helped build the enormously successful Haynes Publishing Group. (You might have a manual for your vehicle?)

A collector of cars and vehicles, John had a special desire to start his own museum. After losing track of where all his cars were, he began to look for a suitable place to store them.

John's impressive collection was housed in a Second World War American munitions dump in Sparkford, Somerset. Because the collection would be available to the public in one place, the future of the collection was protected. On July 10, 1985 the museum opened. Since then, the international theme of the collection has broadened to include exhibits from around the world, bringing in a remarkable 400 vehicles from humble beginnings of just 29 cars 30 years ago.

Fleet Air Arm

RNAS Yeovilton, Ilchester BA22 8HW
www.fleetairarm.com

The museum is dedicated to representing the Royal Navy in the air.

Glastonbury

This compact Somerset town is a centre of New Age culture, rumoured to be the final resting place of King Arthur, and most famously, home to the legendary Glastonbury festival, 'Glasto,' as it is affectionately known, the world-famous 5-day music and arts spectacle.

Glastonbury, with its incense-scented mix of English charm, alternative culture, and eye-opening history, is a joy to visit at any time of year. Explore the quirky, independent stores that sell everything from crystals to organic beauty products. Why not climb Glastonbury Tor for the views, then visit the holy Chalice Well, which is surrounded by peaceful gardens.

The fabled Isle of Avalon, King Arthur's final resting place, is thought to be located near Glastonbury Abbey.

Some believe that Joseph of Arimathea came to Britain from the Holy Land, bringing the Holy Grail with him and founding the first church in the country.

As Arthurian fans will recall, the Holy Grail becomes an important part of King Arthur's story when the knights are sent on a quest to find it. In the 12th century, monks claimed to have discovered the remains of King Arthur and Guinevere, but this was later proven to be a medieval legend created to boost visitor numbers! It is now a romantic ruin in the heart of Glastonbury, surrounded by lovely parkland.

Lytes Cary Manor

Lytes Cary Manor [NT]

Somerton, Somerset, TA11 7HU
www.nationaltrust.org.uk

A medieval manor house with beautiful grounds. It was originally the family home of Henry Lyte, who translated the unique 'Niewe Herball Book on Herbal Remedies', and was lovingly restored by Sir Walter Jenner in the 20th century. The garden room features topiary and floral borders, and the estate's peaceful walks border the River Cary.

Lydford-on-Fosse

The village takes its name from two Saxon words, Lyd meaning a torrent or noisy stream and ford a passage crossing a river. The granting of a charter for a fair and weekly market in the reign of Henry III (1216–1272) suggests that Lydford was already a place of some importance at that time. The modern A37 trunk road follows the Fosse route through the parish.

East Somerset Railway

Cranmore Station, Shepton Mallet BA4 4QP
www.eastsomersetrailway.com

Just outside Shepton Mallet, the railway welcomes steam railway enthusiasts, children, and families alike. Take a train ride and visit the museum, waiting room, and ticket office to learn about the world of steam restoration in action.

Llamafish Wiki Commons

Shepton Mallet

Shepton Mallet is a market town with a colourful history, located at the entrance to the Mendip Hills, an area of outstanding natural beauty. The town is an excellent starting point for exploring the surrounding undulating countryside, which are crisscrossed with trails, footpaths, and the ruins of ancient and medieval industry and workings. Once an important Roman route centre, the town has its own rich history. Shepton Mallet Prison, once the oldest in the country, housed the Kray Twins, the Domesday Book, and the Magna Carta during WWII.

Kinver Court Gardens

Kinver Court Gardens

Kilver St, Shepton Mallet, Somerset BA4 5NF
www.kilvercourt.com/garden

Kilver Court Gardens & nursery in Somerset is tucked away behind vast stone textile mills and beautifully framed by the sweeping curve of the listed Charlton Viaduct. The three-and-a-half-acre garden has appeared on BBC shows such as Gardeners' World.

Shepton Mallet Prison

Frithfield Ln, Shepton Mallet, Somerset BA4 5LU
www.visitsomerset.co.uk

Shepton Mallet was the oldest working prison in the United Kingdom, built in 1610 in response to King James I's Act requiring all counties to have their own 'House of Correction.' Shepton Mallet Prison was decommissioned in 2013.

You can walk around the cells while an ex-officer describes what life was like for both the prisoners and the guards throughout history. The prison, which first opened its doors in 1646, was expanded in 1790, with additional construction work taking place in the 1820s and 1830s, including the installation of a treadwheel for those sentenced to hard labour. The prison was closed in 1930 because the number of inmates had decreased.

The prison was reopened as a military prison after the outbreak of World War II. It was first used by the British Army before being taken over by American forces, who built a new execution block to hang condemned prisoners.

Downside Abbey Church

Stratton-on-the-Fosse, Somerset, BA3 4RH
www.downsideabbey.co.uk

This is the impressive gothic style Abbey Church of St Gregory the Great, begun in 1873 and still unfinished. It is a Benedictine monastery. In 2020, the abbey was home to 16 monks. It dominates the village with its 180 ft tower.

Stratton-on-the-Fosse

Another village that straddles the Fosse Way, and part of the once-thriving Somerset coalfield. Coal was mined from the 15th century until 1973. It is part of a larger coalfield that extends all the way into southern Gloucestershire.

The Somerset coalfield covered an area of about 240 square miles, stretching from Cromhall in the north to the Mendip Hills in the south, and from Bath in the east to Nailsea in the west. There is evidence that the romans mined coal in the area too.

Radstock

Radstock has a long history dating back to the Iron Age. Its significance grew following the completion of the Fosse Way. The town grew rapidly after 1763, when coal was discovered in the area. Coal extraction was difficult due to the complex geology and narrow

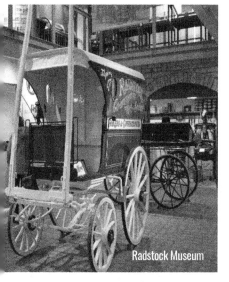

Radstock Museum

seams. Several mines were established during the 19th century, including several owned by the Waldegrave family, Lords of the Manor since the English Civil War. Coal extraction increased throughout the 1800s, peaking in 1901.

There were 79 different collieries with a total annual output of 1.25 million tonnes. Due to local geological challenges and manpower shortages, the pits began to decline, and by the mid-1930s, only 14 remained. Narrow seams increased the cost of production, limiting profit and investment.

The last two pits were closed in September 1973. because of national competition from more cost-effective coalfields.

Radstock Museum

Waterloo Road, Radstock, BA3 3EP
radstockmuseum.co.uk

The permanent exhibits are spread across two floors of the former Radstock Market Hall, which is now a listed building. It tells the story of the Somerset coalmines, the mining communities of Radstock, and the local trades and industries that supported them. A candle-lit coalmine depicts how dangerous and difficult it was for men and boys as young as five years old to work in Somerset's famously narrow coal seams, which were sometimes only two feet high. There are also glimpses into how a miner's wife managed her day-to-day life while raising up to 14 children in a small cottage.

Stoney Littleton Long Barrow [EH]

Wellow, Somerset, BA2 8NR
www.english-heritage.org.uk

Stoney Littleton Long Barrow is one of the best examples of a Neolithic chambered tomb in England. It is 30 metres long, dates from around 3500 BC, and has multiple burial chambers open to the public. One mile from Wellow, there is a small free car park off Littleton Lane, and the barrow is signposted from there. It is important to note that the walk is a moderate climb with three stiles to cross. The route can be exposed and muddy in places, so dress appropriately.

Combe Down Tunnel

Near Brassmill Lane, Bath
(No postcode see instructions)
www.twotunnels.org.uk

Combe Down Tunnel is the UK's longest cycling and walking tunnel. Opened in 2013, you can make your way alongside the steel rails that once guided trains on the Somerset and Dorset line to the south coast. The relatively flat route takes you past Bath's Georgian crescents before leaving the city and entering the beautiful countryside south of the city. Leaving the houses behind, you'll travel through the dramatic, curved tunnel, emerging in a deep wooded valley that feels far from the city centre—though, with Bath Spa Station just over half a mile away, you might hear the trains.

Before visiting, it's suggested you read the Two Tunnels code of conduct available on the website. (www.two-tunnels.org.uk/code-of-conduct.html.) Note: It can be tricky to find. The Newbridge Park and Ride (BA1 3NB) is recommended. Leave your car at the park and ride and head east along the Upper Bristol Road towards the city. Take the first right (Brassmill Lane) then on to the river towpath. Lastly, following signs, cross the green steel footbridge over the river.

Prior Park Landscaped Gardens [NT]

Ralph Allen Dr, Bath, BA2 5AH
www.nationaltrust.org.uk

Prior Park was built in the 18th century by local entrepreneur Ralph Allen with the guidance of 'Capability' Brown and poet Alexander Pope. Visitors can enjoy magnificent views and are just a stone's throw away from the Bath Skyline—a six-mile circular route encompassing beautiful woodlands and meadows, an Iron Age hill fort, Roman settlements, 18th century follies, and spectacular views. Get away from it all with a stroll through an immaculately designed 18th century landscaped garden. Explore lakes and winding wooded paths and cross the famous Palladian Bridge, one of only three bridges of its kind in the UK.

The dams are being restored (2021), giving visitors the opportunity to see how 18th century landscape engineering is getting some TLC.

NOTE: While the restoration works take place, there is no onsite parking. The trust suggests getting a bus from the city centre.

A Palladian bridge at Prior Park

Bath Park & Ride

(South) Odd Down Park off the A367, Bath BA2 2SL

(West) Newbridge, Bath BA1 3NB

(North) Lansdown Park, Lansdown, Bath BA1 9BJ

travelwest.info/park-ride

An easy, cheap, and convenient way to park up and take the bus into Bath.

Bath

Aqua Sulis

Bath, built for pleasure and relaxation, has been a wellbeing destination since Roman times. The waters are still popular, both at the ancient Roman Baths and at the modern Thermae Bath Spa, which currently houses the only natural thermal hot springs in Britain that can be bathed in.

The honey-coloured Georgian architecture looks straight out of a Jane Austen novel, with highlights including the iconic Royal Crescent and the majestic Circus.

Bath's compact, visitor-friendly centre is brimming with places to eat and drink, as well as some of the best independent shops in the country, making it ideal for a city break. Immerse yourself in the extraordinary collection of museums and galleries.

Archaeological evidence shows that the site of the Roman baths' main spring may have been treated as a shrine by the Britons, and was dedicated to the goddess Sulis, whom the Romans identified with Minerva; the name Sulis continued to be used after the Roman invasion, appearing in the town's Roman name, Aquae Sulis (literally, 'the waters of Sulis').

A temple was constructed in AD 60–70, and a bathing complex was built up over the next 300 years. According to the Victorian churchman Edward Churton, during the Anglo-Saxon era, Bath was known as Acemannesceastre ('Akemanchester'), or 'aching men's city', on account of the reputation these springs had for healing the sick.

Edgar of England was crowned king of England in Bath Abbey in 973, in a ceremony that formed the basis of all future English coronations.

William Rufus granted the town, abbey and mint to a royal physician, John of Tours, who became Bishop of Wells and Abbot of Bath, following the sacking of the town during the rebellion of 1088.

Much of the creamy gold Bath stone, a type of limestone used for construction in the city, was obtained from the Combe Down and Bathampton Down Mines owned by Ralph Allen (1694–1764). Allen, to advertise the quality of his quarried limestone, commissioned the elder John Wood to build a country house on his Prior Park estate between the city and the mines. Allen was elected mayor for a single term in 1742.

During World War II, between the evening of April 25 and the early morning of April 27 1942, Bath suffered three air raids in reprisal for RAF raids on the German cities of Lübeck and Rostock, part of the Luftwaffe campaign also known as the 'Baedeker Blitz'.

During the Bath Blitz, more than 400 people were killed, and more than 19,000 buildings damaged or destroyed. Houses in Royal Crescent, Circus and Paragon were burnt out along with the Assembly Rooms.

A post-war review of inadequate housing led to the clearance and redevelopment of areas of the city in a post-war style, often at variance with the local Georgian style.

The Roman Baths

Roman Baths

Abbey Church Yard, Bath BA1 1LZ
www.romanbaths.co.uk

Immerse yourself in history and see how Bath's former residents relaxed all those centuries ago. Interactive exhibits and CGI reconstructions bring this unique ancient site back to life, showing how important the baths were to our Roman ancestors.

Bath Abbey

8 Kingston Buildings, Bath, BA1 1LT
www.bathabbey.org

There has been a place of worship on this spot for more than 1,000 years (King Edgar, the first king of all England, was crowned here in 973 AD), but many of the present-day Abbey's most spectacular features are more recent. Bath Abbey's spectacular Victorian Gothic interior is the work of Sir George Gilbert Scott, who made numerous improvements between 1864 and 1874, including the addition of the soaring vaulted stone ceiling above the nave.

Mary Shelley's House of Frankenstein

37 Gay Street, Bath, BA1 2NT
www.houseoffrankenstein.com

Step into the dark world of Mary Shelley and her greatest creation, Frankenstein. Extending over four atmospheric floors, including their dank foreboding basement, immerse yourself in the author's complex and often tragic past, and uncover the true story behind the world's favourite monster.

Bath Abbey

Holburne Museum

Great Pulteney Street, Bath, BA2 4DB
www.www.holburne.org

At the heart of the Holburne Museum is the collection of Sir William Holburne (1793-1874), 5th baronet of Menstrie. William seemed destined for a naval career but, following the death of his elder brother Francis, he inherited the family title and a modest fortune. He left the navy and embarked on an 18-month grand tour of Europe, visiting Italy, the Alps, and the Netherlands. This sparked a life-long interest in art and his enthusiasm for collecting.

Sir William never married. He lived with his growing collection and his three unmarried sisters on the North side of Bath. It was his wish that his collection be left to the City of Bath for everyone to enjoy. Since his death, more than 2,000 items have been added to his collection including portrait miniatures, porcelain, embroideries, and portraits by some of the greatest artists of the 18th century.

Bath Postal Museum

27 Northgate Street, Bath BA1 1AJ
bathpostalmuseum.org.uk

Visit Bath Postal Museum to learn more about Bath's role in the development of the modern postal system. Their colourful and frequently-changing exhibitions tell the story of influential figures such as Ralph Allen and John Palmer. Play interactive games and quizzes, take a close look at models and collectables, and learn from historic 'talking heads' video characters. There are also many fun activities for children.

Pulteney Bridge

Bridge Street, Bath, BA2 4AT

Completed in 1774, Pulteney Bridge brings a touch of Italy to Bath. Inspired by Ponte Vecchio in Florence and lined by shops on both sides, it is one of only four such structures in the world. Viewed from across the river, the bridge's elegant arches are complemented by the curved cascades of the weir just downstream. It looks magical lit up at night.

Jane Austen Centre

40 Gay Street, Bath BA1 2NT
www.janeausten.co.uk

Celebrating Bath's most famous resident, the centre offers a snapshot of what it would be like to live in the Regency era—the fashion, food, society—everything that would have inspired Austen's timeless novels. Explore how the city of Bath impacted upon Jane Austen's life and writing.

Victoria Art Gallery

Bridge Street, Bath BA2 4AT
www.victoriagal.org.uk

A public art museum and home to a diverse collection of paintings, sculptures, and decorative arts. Included in the many items in its care are an original Tudor portrait of Henry VIII in the style of Holbein and works by Thomas Gainsborough and Grayson Perry.

Herschel Museum of Astronomy

19 New King St, Bath BA1 2BL
www.herschelmuseum.org.uk

This residence is where, in March 1781, the German-born British astronomer William Herschel discovered the planet Uranus. Even more remarkable, is that Herschel was a self-taught astronomer, who built his own telescopes at home. As well as discovering a new planet, he noted the rotation of Saturn's rings, identified satellites of Saturn and other planets. Through his observations of the sun, he also detected the existence of infrared radiation—an energy source now used to power modern space missions. William was awarded the title of King's Astronomer and went on to build a series of even larger telescopes. In an age where scientific opportunities for women were few, he publicly acknowledged his sister Caroline as his 'astronomical assistant'. She went on to gain a reputation as a pioneering astronomer in her own right and was paid for her scientific work. She discovered eight comets (one of which is named after her) and won a gold medal from the Royal Astronomical Society.

Alexandra Park

56 Alexandra Park, Bath BA2 4RQ
visitbath.co.uk

The Bath Lookout at Alexandra Park is perched on the summit of a wooded hill overlooking the city. It's accessible by car or bus, or by climbing the zig-zag path that rewards your efforts with stunning vistas of the city and surrounding countryside once you reach the top.

Tourists on a bus

Open Top Bus Tour

Multiple stops around the city
www.city-sightseeing.com/bath

A sightseeing tour through Bath on the distinctive red buses is a fantastic way to experience this incredible city, visiting many of the most prominent attractions in a short period of time. (Plus, it's a break from driving yourself everywhere!) The tour includes two routes that allow you to explore both the city and the countryside. The City Route, with 17 stops, takes you to all the city's historic sites. Enjoy the panoramic view from the open-top red buses. Hop on and off at your leisure. It is a stunning tour through beautiful countryside and takes in some of the most spectacular views Bath has to offer. Two easy to find stops are Bath Abbey and Bath railway station.

STAGE 3

BATH TO CIRENCESTER

42 Miles

Take in the majesty of the Cotswolds and visit Corinium, the second largest Roman settlement after Londinium.

THE ROUTE

EXETER TO LINCOLN		LINCOLN TO EXETER	
↳ 0m	Bath	↳ 0m	Cirencester
↳ 11m	Corsham (A4)	↳ 14m	Malmesbury (A429)
↳ 3m	Chippenham (A4)	↳ 7m	Stanton St Quintin (A429)
↳ 5m	Stanton St Quintin (A350)	↳ 5m	Chippenham (A350)
↳ 7m	Malmesbury (A429)	↳ 3m	Corsham (A4)
↳ 14m	Cirencester (A429)	↳ 11m	Bath (A4)

Burford

A40

A4095

A361

A420

A415

A420

Bampton

R Thames
or Isis

OXFORDSH

Abingdon-
on-Thames

Faringdon

Highworth

9

Wantage

A417

A338

A34

Did

Blewb

Swindon

15

Lambourn

East
Ilsley

Go

A346

WEST BERKSHIRE

NDON

ry

Marlborough

S

14

M4

13

S

A4

Thatc

Newb

Hungerford

A338

Ta

A339

A346

Burbage

Pewsey

A342

A343

A34

Basingst

Ludgershall

Whitchurch

A338

A345

Tidworth

Plain

Andover

A303

Browns Folly Nature Reserve

1 Prospect Pl, Bathford, Bath BA1 7TW
www.avonwildlifetrust.org.uk

Standing high above the River Avon with commanding views towards Bath, Browne's Folly boasts flower-rich grasslands and ancient woodland on the remains of old Bath stone quarries, which has been designated as a SSSI.

Corsham Court

Church St, Corsham, Wilts, SN13 0BZ
www.corsham-court.co.uk

Corsham Court is an English country house in a park designed by Capability Brown. In the days of the Saxon kings, Corsham was a royal manor, rumoured to have been a seat of Ethelred the Unready. Following William the Conqueror, the manor was passed down through the royal family's generations. During the 16th century, the manor was owned by two of Henry VIII's wives: Catherine of Aragon until 1536 and Katherine Parr until 1548. During Elizabeth I's reign, the estate passed out of the royal family. The current house was built in 1582 by Thomas Smythe. Sir Paul Methuen purchased the house in 1745 for his cousin, also named Paul Methuen. The Methuen family still lives in the house.

Corsham Court

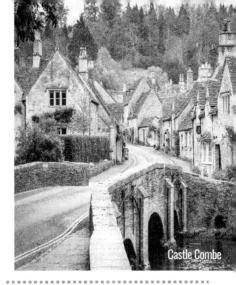
Castle Combe

Castle Combe

Castle Combe, Wiltshire SN14 7NG
www.visitwiltshire.co.uk

A quintessential English village in the Wiltshire Cotswolds, the houses are made of the honey-coloured Cotswold stone typical of this area. Stop at the bottom of the village by the bridge for a great photo opportunity.

It gets its name from an abandoned 12th century castle about 500 metres to the north. A Roman villa stood about three miles from the village centuries ago. A bath house and corn drying ovens were discovered. The villa had around 16 rooms. There were additional buildings and a cemetery. The market cross was built in the 14th century when the right to hold a weekly market was granted. It reflects the importance of the textile industry in this region. Horse riders could mount and dismount on small stone steps near the cross. One of two water pumps is located next to the cross.

The village had a wool mill by 1340. Alas, the River Bybrook's level fell sometime in the late 1700s, and it could no longer power the mills. The textile industry began to leave the area. The industrial boom had ended, and the population had shrunk.

Castle Combe Circuit

Chippenham, Wiltshire SN14 7EY
castlecombecircuit.co.uk

Castle Combe Circuit opened in the summer of 1950, just 18 months after Silverstone, making it one of the UK's oldest circuits. A young Stirling Moss won a race that first year, and over the next few years, names like Mike Hawthorn, Colin Chapman, Les Leston, Roy Salvadori, and John Surtees wowed huge crowds. In 1976, the long road to developing the circuit as a modern national racing venue began. In the 1970s and 1980s, Nigel Mansell, Ayrton Senna, and David Coulthard all won races, and by the 1990s, the circuit had hosted rounds of most national championships. The site offers track days, race days and experiences.

Malmesbury

Malmesbury, another market town, rose to prominence as a centre of learning during the Middle Ages, thanks to its abbey. Once the site of an Iron Age fort, it became the site of a monastery famous for its teaching quality and one of Alfred the Great's fortified burhs for defence against the Vikings during the Anglo-Saxon period. When Athelstan, the first king of England, died in 939, he was buried in Malmesbury Abbey.

Athelstan Museum

Cross Hayes, Malmesbury SN16 9BZ
www.athelstanmuseum.org.uk

Housed in the town hall, Athelstan Museum tells the history of Malmesbury.

Find out about the fine and intricate Malmesbury Lace and learn about the Abbey, from its architecture to its long history, including how it encouraged the growth of the town. The displays also include a Roman coffin.

Malmesbury Abbey

Holloway, Malmesbury SN16 9BA
www.malmesburyabbey.com

Malmesbury Abbey was constructed in the 1200s. Celtic pilgrims and Benedictine monks shaped its history. It is an important reformation survivor.

See King Athelstan's tomb, a 15th century illuminated bible, Henry VII's crest, a Norman porch depicting Christian salvation history, and the gravestone of Hannah Twynnoy, a local girl killed in 1703 by a tiger kept as an exhibit in the nearby pub where she worked. Also discover that Eilmer of Malmesbury was the country's first aviator who took flight in something resembling a hang glider around 1005.

Malmesbury

The Abbey House Gardens

Market Cross, Malmesbury SN16 9AS
www.abbeyhousegardens.co.uk

Steeped in over 1,000 years of history, with an English King's burial place, knot gardens, herb gardens, river walk, monastic fish ponds and a waterfall. The impressive garden has over 2,000 different roses, the largest collection in the UK. There are over 100,000 tulips, and 10,000 different plants, providing constant colour from March to November. These 5 acres are a must-see location for garden fans.

Charlton Park Estate

Malmesbury, Wiltshire, SN16 9DG
charltonparkestate.com

Charlton Park has been in the hands of the Earls of Suffolk since the late 16th century. The estate is 4,500 acres and includes the impressive Grade I-listed Mansion.

Chippenham

Settlements in the Chippenham area are thought to have existed before Roman times. There are Roman remains in the wall behind the former magistrates' court. The Saxon town is thought to have been founded around AD 600.

In 878, Danish Vikings successfully besieged Chippenham. Later that year, at the Battle of Ethandun, Alfred decisively defeated the Danes.

The A4 incorporates parts of the 14th century medieval road network that connected London to Bristol. It was a

Chippenham

vital route for the English cloth trade, and the Bristol merchants contributed to its upkeep. In 1611 and 1636, the town was devastated by the plague. This, combined with a downturn in the woollen industry and a drop in corn production in 1622 and 1623, resulted in severe hardship for the town's population.

In 1841, the Great Western Railway, attracted a slew of new businesses and a spate of house building. The arrival of the railway aided the expansion of industrial agricultural businesses. Chippenham was a major centre in the production of dairy and ham products in the mid-nineteenth century, leading to Nestlé and Matteson's having factories in the town centre.

Eddie Cochran was killed in a car accident on Rowden Hill in Chippenham on April 17, 1960. A memorial plaque was erected near the scene.

Tetbury

Tetbury is built on the site of an ancient hill fort, on which an Anglo-Saxon monastery was founded around 681. It was another major market for Cotswold wool and yarn during the

Middle Ages. It is the second largest town in the Cotswolds and the residence of the Prince of Wales.

The centre contains many fine stone buildings in a variety of styles that reflect architectural trends over the last 400 years. Many of these fine homes were originally built and financed by wool merchants, although Tetbury never produced cloth because it lacked continuous running water to service mills.

St Mary's Church's impressive spire can be seen from all directions. The nave of the church was built in the late 1770s to replace a medieval church, and the tower and spire were rebuilt about a century later. The interior, with its perpendicular layout and high box pews, is light and airy and must be seen.

Chipping Steps, located in the corner of The Chipping car park, is an old entrance to the town, and the picturesque cottages that run down the side were most likely weaver's cottages.

Tetbury's centre is a conservation area, and many of its buildings have graded listing. Look up as you walk the streets to see the Cotswolds' famous architecture and natural stone.

Tetbury Town Hall

Cotswold Airport

Cirencester, Glos, GL7 6BA
www.cotswoldairport.com

Cotswold Airport was once known as RAF Kemble. It has become a busy private airport for microlights, general aviation, corporate aircraft, and airliners. The airport is open to the public and has a restaurant with views of the runway from its south-facing sun terrace. The Fosse runs through parts of it.

Cotswold Sculpture Park

Somerford Keynes, Glos, GL7 6FE
cotswoldsculpturepark.co.uk

The Cotswold Sculpture Park is in a 10-acre site that has been transformed into a mixed deciduous and conifer woodland complete with ponds, gardens, and glades. These diverse spaces are connected by meandering paths that take you on a journey around the park, which serves as a restful outdoor backdrop for contemporary art.

Cirencester

CORINIUM DOBUNNORUM

Roman Corinium Dobunnorum was the second largest town in Britain after Londinium. Cirencester, also known as the Cotswolds' capital, was the second largest town in Britain during the
Roman period. Later, it became a prosperous medieval wool town. The cathedral-like Parish Church of St. John Baptist dominates Cirencester's market square (one of the largest in England). Around 1490, the large

south porch with its impressive fan vaulting was built.

Cirencester's status as a market town was mentioned in the Domesday Book. Traders continue to set up their stalls, and the town has had its own farmers' market since 1999. Craft and antique markets are also popular draws. Henry the 4th Earl Bathurst, who later became the founding president of the Royal College of Agriculture in Cirencester, established the first agricultural college in the English-speaking world in 1840. The college was founded to train young farmers in the best agricultural methods available at the time and to lead the way in terms of innovation.

Amphitheatre [EH]

Cotswold Ave, Cirencester, Glos GL7 1XW
www.english-heritage.org.uk

The second largest in Britain, it indicates the site's importance during Roman times. It had an arena approximately 150 feet long, 135 feet wide, and 25 feet deep. The earthworks show evidence of 8000-capacity tiered wooden seats, placed on stone terraces, though a timber-only structure may have existed before. During the 5th century, the amphitheatre was fortified to defend against invading Saxons. Wooden structures were erected and placed in postholes within the arena, and the north-east entrance was partially blocked. It was also known as the 'Bull Ring,' because it was used for baiting.

Corinium Museum

Park Street, Cirencester, Glos, GL7 2BX
coriniummuseum.org

The museum's main collection consists of important finds from the Roman town. It also traces the evolution of the Cotswolds from the prehistoric era to the present.

The Church of St John the Baptist

5 Market Pl, Cirencester, Glos GL7 2NX
www.cirenparish.co.uk

This is a grade I listed famous for its perpendicular porch, fan vaulted ceilings, medieval glass, wall paintings, and merchants' tombs, as well as being one of England's largest parish churches. Like many in the area it was funded by the wool trade. The chancel is the oldest part of the structure, and the current church was built on the site of an earlier, Saxon church in the 12th century. It was widened around 1180. The nave was completely rebuilt around 1240. The east window was built around 1300. Following the town's skirmishes during the English Civil War in 1642, the church was used to imprison local citizens overnight.

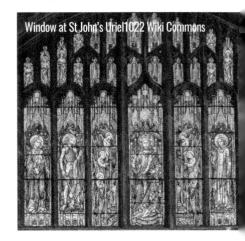
Window at St John's Uriel1022 Wiki Commons

STAGE 4

CIRENCESTER TO LEICESTER
80 Miles

Take in a string of breath-taking Cotswold villages, then enjoy the Fosse as it follows some quiet Leicestershire B-roads.

THE ROUTE

EXETER TO LINCOLN

- ⤵ 0m Cirencester
- ⤵ 11m Northleach (A429)
- ⤵ 6m Bourton-on-the-Water (A429)
- ⤵ 4m Stow-on-the-Wold (A429)
- ⤵ 4m Moreton-in-Marsh (A429)
- ⤵ 9m Halford (A429)
- ⤵ 18m Wappenbury (B4455)
- ⤵ 17m Sharnford (B4114)
- ⤵ 10m Leicester (A5460)

LINCOLN TO EXETER

- ⤵ 0m Leicester
- ⤵ 10m Sharnford (A5460)
- ⤵ 17m Wappenbury (B4114)
- ⤵ 18m Halford (B4455)
- ⤵ 9m Moreton-in-Marsh (A429)
- ⤵ 4m Stow-on-the-Wold (A429)
- ⤵ 4m Bourton-on-the-Water (A429)
- ⤵ 6m Northleach (A429)
- ⤵ 11m Cirencester (A429)

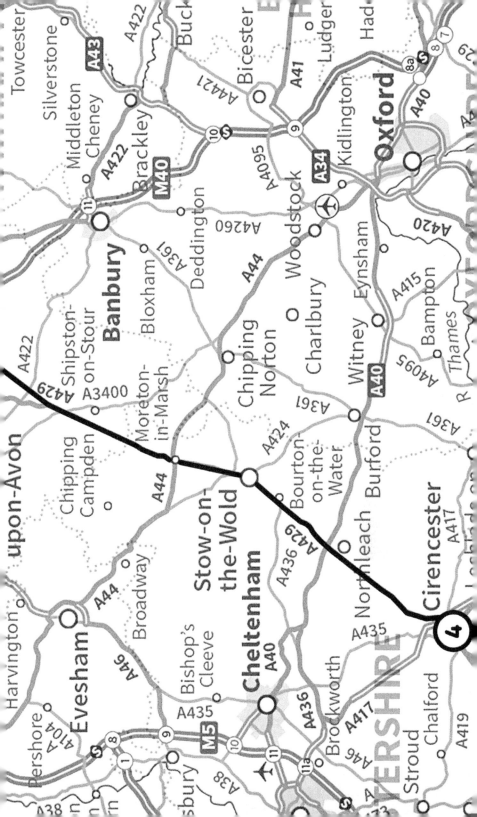

Northleach

Northleach

Gloucestershire, GL54 3EG
www.cotswolds.com

Northleach's streets, tucked away from the busy A40, are rich in architectural interest, ranging from half-timbered buildings and merchants' houses from the 15th and 16th centuries to the 18th century 'House of Correction' built at the crossroads. The Old Prison has been converted into a café. Apart from more 'recent' additions of late 16th- and 17th century buildings surrounded the green to form the town centre, Market Place, has remained compact and completely unchanged since 1500. Walking through the small alleys, you'll see houses with upper levels of timber framing that overhang great stone-built walls and wide oak doors. It is also home to the Cotswold Discovery Centre.

Chedworth Roman Villa [NT]

Yanworth, Gloucestershire, GL54 3LJ
www.nationaltrust.org.uk

One of the largest and most elaborate Roman villas ever discovered in Britain. It was developed in stages from the early 2nd to the 5th century. In the 4th century, it was made into an elite dwelling arranged around three sides of a courtyard. The heated and furnished west wing included a dining room with a fine mosaic floor, as well as two separate bathing suites: one for damp-heat and one for dry-heat. Discovered in 1863, it was soon excavated and displayed.

Cheltenham

A little way off the Fosse route but worth a visit. Following the discovery of mineral springs in 1716, Cheltenham became known as a health and holiday spa town resort. It claims to be the most complete British Regency town.

Royal Crescent, Cheltenh

Villa mosaic Matt Gibson Flickr

Lodge Park [NT]

Aldsworth, Gloucestershire, GL54 3DT
www.nationaltrust.org.uk

This 17th century grandstand was built by John 'Crump' Dutton, who was inspired by his love of deer coursing, gambling, banqueting, and entertaining. In 1720s the building was remodelled and new stone floors were added, and plasterwork ceiling in the Great Room. In the 19th century, it was modified into a house, then a row of cottages, and then into a house again.

Bourton-On-The-Water

Bourton's High Street is bordered by lush, broad greens and the River Windrush, which runs between them. The river is crossed by five low, arched stone bridges. They were built between 1654 and 1953, earning Bourton the nickname 'Venice of the Cotswolds.'

Icknield Street was another Roman road that connected Bourton-on-the-Water's Fosse Way to Templeborough in South Yorkshire. The discovery of ancient Roman pottery and coins in the village itself demonstrates the long Roman occupation of the village.

Around AD 708, a Saxon timber church was constructed on the site of an old Roman temple. By the 11th century, the Norman Christian church of St Lawrence had been established, and the village developed in much the same way that it does today along the River Windrush. It was developed further in the 17th and 18th centuries.

Model Village

Rissington Rd, Bourton, Glos GL54 2AF
theoldnewinn.co.uk

Explore the country's only Grade II-listed model village. Made from local Cotswold stone by highly skilled craftsmen, it is a replica of the buildings that existed in Bourton-on-the-Water in the 1930s and shows how they are used today, as banks, shops, meeting halls and more.

The Dragonfly Maze

Rissington Rd, Bourton, Glos GL54 2BN
thedragonflymaze.com

The Dragonfly Maze, which first opened in 1997, is a traditional yew hedge maze with a twist. It's all about finding the maze's centre, home to the golden dragonfly, solving puzzles along the way. Kit Williams created the maze. He first came to public attention in 1979 when his treasure hunt book 'Masquerade' was published. It challenged the curious reader to find a 'golden hare' buried somewhere in the English countryside. The dragonfly itself was made with gold and semi-precious stones left over from William's original golden hare.

Bourton-on-the-Water

Cotswold Motoring Museum

Bourton, Glos, GL54 2BY
www.cotswoldmotoringmuseum.co.uk

Explore the history of 20th century automobiles on a fascinating journey through time. This collection of rare vintage vehicles and memorabilia will transport you back to a simpler motoring era when life on the road was simpler.

The Old Mill Museum

Mill Lane, Lower Slaughter, Glos, GL54 2HX
oldmill-lowerslaughter.com

A historic mill with a museum in the picturesque village of Lower Slaughter. Since the Domesday book, there has been a mill in this location. It is located on the River Eye. See the inner workings of the mill machinery and exhibits about the history of bread making

Stow-on-the-Wold

Stow-On-The-Wold

Stow-on-the-Wold is the tallest of the Cotswold towns, perched on the 800-foot-high Stow Hill at the crossroads of eight major roads, including the Fosse Way. At the height of the Cotswold wool industry, the town was famous for its massive annual fairs, where up to 20,000 sheep could be sold at once. The expansive market square attests to the town's former importance. The ancient cross stands at one end, and the town stocks are at the other, shaded by an old elm tree. The square is surrounded by an elegant collection of Cotswold town houses and shops.

Its location on the crossroads of the major thoroughfares meant the royalist and parliamentary armies frequently passed through the town. The Battle of Stow-on-the-Wold, the last of the Civil War, took place on 21 March 1646.

In more recent times, on July 10, 2002, the funeral of John Entwistle, the famous bass guitarist of The Who, was held at St Edward's church.

Look out for the visitor centre, based in St Edward's Hall for more information about the town.

This church was built on the site of an earlier Saxon church between the 11th and 15th centuries, with additional expansions and repairs in Victorian times. The 88-foot-tall, four-stage tower, constructed in 1447, stands out as a prominent landmark adorned with pinnacles and gargoyles. The pair of ancient yew trees flanking the 17th or 18th century north porch are a remarkable external feature of St Edward's. Fierce debate rages about whether the doorway inspired Tolkien or not...

The ancient stocks (or their remains) can be found on the market square's north side. Stocks were used as a form of public humiliation and corporal punishment in the medieval period. Victims were partially immobilised by the stocks, with their feet locked in them, and then subjected to the scorn of onlookers. This contempt was frequently shown by hurling rotten food at the pinned victim.

Hawk in flight

Cotswold Falconry Centre

Batsford, Glos GL56 9AT
www.cotswold-falconry.co.uk

Flying displays are held at the centre, which houses over 130 birds of 60 species. Learn about how different species hunt and catch their prey, as well as the skill sets that make them successful predators, in a close environment. Take a stroll through the breeding aviaries in between displays. Some critically endangered birds can also be found at the centre. CCTV cameras installed at many of the nesting sites provide an even closer look at what is going on.

Moreton-In-Marsh

Moreton-in-Marsh received its market charter in 1227. It grew into a substantial town with a broad main street, narrow rented 'burbage' plots of land, and tiny back lanes.

Moreton was established on the Fosse, and later the London-to-Worcestershire coaching route via Broadway. It has been a traveller's town for at least 1700 years and served as a coaching station prior to the arrival of the Oxford to Worcester railway line in 1853.

Many of the historic structures on the High Street date from the 17th and 18th centuries, including elegant 18th century inns and houses, as well as the Redesdale Market Hall. The oldest structure is most likely the 16th century Curfew tower on High Street.

Redesdale Hall, an impressive Tudor style grade II listed building was designed by the architect Sir Ernest George and built in 1887.

The Parish Church of St. David was rebuilt in medieval style in 1858.

The Tolkien rumours resurface here as well. The author is thought to have had ties to Moreton-in-Marsh; a branch of the Tolkien Society presented a special print to a pub in the town. After extensive research, the Society claims that The Bell Inn was the inspiration for The Prancing Pony, Middle Earth's most famous pub in the book 'Lord of the Rings.'

Curfew Tower

4c Oxford St, Moreton, GL56 OLE
historicengland.org.uk

The Curfew Tower in Moreton is one of the town's oldest structures, and it would have played an important role in the settlement's life from the 16th century onward. It faces the market place and is known to have served as a jail for local drunks and minor criminals for much of its history because there was no other option for their confinement within the town. Its bell was rung every night until 1860 to warn people of the dangers of fire at night. It is said that it once guided Sir Robert Fry home after he became lost in the fog, and in gratitude, he donated money for its upkeep.

Batsford Arboretum and Garden Centre

Batsford, Moreton, Glos, GL56 9AT
www.batsarb.co.uk

The Batsford collections include plants from all over the world, with a focus on the Far East. There are over 2,850 labelled specimens, which include approximately 1,300 different trees, shrubs, and bamboo.

Statue at Batsford Arboretum

Wellington Aviation

Bourton Rd, Moreton. Glos GL56 OHB
www.wellingtonaviation.org

Five minutes' walk from the High Street, the museum is housed in a section of an old Victorian schoolhouse. It contains a treasure trove of RAF memorabilia and aviation art. The extensive private collection has become an invaluable record of how the Second World War impacted a small market town, including the 'Wings for Victory' appeal, local prisoner of war camps, and the encampment of the United States Army prior to the D Day landings.

British Motor Museum

Banbury Rd, Gaydon, Warks CV35 OBJ
britishmotormuseum.co.uk

The British motor industry has been a vital part of the economy and the lives of people living in the Midlands since its inception, and it is still a hub for automotive creativity today. This

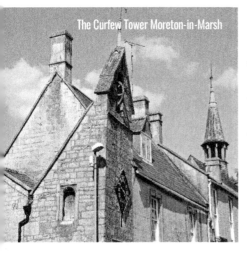
The Curfew Tower Moreton-in-Marsh

museum tells the story of the birth, decline, and rebirth of the automobile industry and the vehicles it produced, as well as the skills and creativity of those who designed and built them. Explore over 300 classic cars from the collections of the British Motor Industry Heritage Trust and the Jaguar Heritage Trust. Learn about the people who built the cars, the locations where they were built, and the stories the guides must tell. Family-friendly interactive displays also bring the subject to life.

Sezincote House

Moreton-in-Marsh, Glos GL56 9AW
www.sezincote.co.uk

Sezincote is a unique country home. The design is in the Rajasthani Mogul style, with a central dome, minarets, peacock-tail windows, jali-work railings, and pavilions. The Persian Garden of Paradise, with its fountain and canals, is framed by a curving orangery. The house is set in a romantic garden with pools, waterfalls, a grotto, and a temple to the Hindu Sun God, which is a fine example of the picturesque style. Sezincote was built by Charles Cockerell, who had previously worked in India, with the help of his architect brother, and Thomas Daniell, the great painter of Indian architectural scenery. The gardens were designed with the help of Humphrey Repton. Some say Sezincote influenced the design of the Brighton pavilion after a visit by The Prince Regent in 1807.

Dorn

Another Roman settlement and the largest of five defended small towns on the line of the Fosse Way between Cirencester and Lincoln.

Stretton-on-Fosse

The name Stretton is derived from the Old English words stræt and tun, which mean 'settlement on a Roman road.' Stratone, as it was known in 1086, is listed in the Domesday Book as having two manors. To this day, these are still two important houses in the area. The current manor house, built in 1886, is a grade II listed structure. Stretton House, also grade II listed, was built in the early 1600s but underwent significant renovations in the early 1800s. Paul De Merry, Lord of Stretton-on-Fosse, holds the second manor and is a direct descendant of Ralph de Toeni, Lord of Flamsted, who held the manor in 1235.

Cottage at Stretton-on-Fosse

Compton Verney

Compton Verney, Warks CV35 9HZ
www.comptonverney.org.uk

This award-winning art gallery is housed in a grade I listed mansion surrounded by 120 acres of Capability Brown-designed grounds. The impressive permanent collections focus on six specific areas that are generally under-represented in other British museums and galleries: 16th century Germanic art; 17th century Neapolitan art; and 18th century British art. There is also British portraiture of Tudor royals and paintings by Sir Joshua Reynolds. Finally, there is the country's largest collection of British folk art, as well as the work of 20th century textile designer Enid Marx.

Charlcote Park [NT]

Wellesbourne, Warks CV35 9ER
www.nationaltrust.org.uk

The Lucy family has lived in Charlcote Park since the 12th century. Their portraits, the objects they collected from all over the world, and the design influence they had on the house and parkland tell their stories throughout the house. See how Mary Elizabeth Lucy remodelled the house in Victorian times. The gardens include a formal parterre, a woodland walk, and the larger parkland (inspired by 'Capability' Brown), which offers walks with picturesque views of the River Avon. Since Tudor times, a herd of fallow deer has roamed the park.

Chesterton

The home of the notable Chesterton Windmill. The parish church dedicated to St Giles is thought to date back to the 12th century. The church used to serve the Chesterton settlement. This settlement vanished as a result of the residents' relocation to Chesterton Green following a visit from that most unwelcome of itinerants, the plague. According to local legend, tunnels connect the church to the nearby Humble Bee cottages (grade II listed but now abandoned.) The Peyto family, who lived at Chesterton House, had owned much of the village since the 1350s. The house was demolished in 1802 after the last of the family, Margaret Peyto, died in 1772 and left

her estates to her cousin John Verney of nearby Compton Verney.

Chesterton Windmill

Windmill Hill Ln, Leamington, Warks CV33 9LB
www.ourwarwickshire.org.uk

A beautiful stone milling machine built in the 1630s. Just off the Fosse Way, it

Chesterton Windmill

was constructed on the site of an earlier mill for Stuart landowner, Sir Edward Peyto, according to a design by Inigo Jones. It was part of a planned landscape associated with the mansion at Chesterton. The domed roof is covered in lead, and designed to revolve to face the wind. The building has been fully restored and much of the original machinery is intact. It is located, aptly, on Windmill Hill.

Uften Field Nature Reserve

Ufton, Southam, Warks CV33 9PU
www.warwickshirewildlifetrust.org.uk

Many unusual plants thrive in this nature reserve, which was formed after limestone excavations ceased. It also has 15 different dragonfly varieties and 28 butterfly species. A mostly flat, circular, waymarked surfaced footpath with signs to guide the way. The reserve is half a mile south of Uften village.

Stratford-Upon-Avon

The town synonymous with the author William Shakespeare. No visit to Stratford would be complete without learning more about the famous English poet and playwright who made the town famous. Shakespeare's birthplace, where he was born and raised, explains more about his early years. Other must-see Shakespeare locations include Hall's Croft, William's daughter's home. Shakespeare's New Place was where he spent the last chapter of his life. Nearby are Anne Hathaway's cottage, a romantic setting, and Mary Arden's Farm, which was his mother's childhood home.

Shakespeare's grave is in the Church of the Holy Trinity. The growing phenomenon of 'bardolotry' (the literary worship of Shakespeare) made

Historic buildings, Stratford-upon-Avon

Stratford a draw for tourists.

It may have started when, over three days in 1769, the actor, theatre owner and playwright, David Garrick staged a major Shakespeare Jubilee. It saw the construction of a large rotunda and brought in a huge influx of visitors, despite being held 205 years after Shakespeare's birth rather than 200.

Warwick

Warwick was founded in 914 AD on the banks of the River Avon by Aethelflaed, daughter of King Alfred, as a defence against Danish invaders. The site overlooked earlier riverside settlements. It is built on a small hill that controls not only the river valley but also the river crossing on the road to London, as well as the roads to Stratford, Coventry, and the salt way to Droitwich, known as Salinae to the Romans. The small Anglo-Saxon town was surrounded by a wall and a ditch. Warwick's impressive castle is one of the most complete medieval one in the country. Continuously inhabited since the Middle Ages, it was the home of the Earls of Warwick until recently, including Richard Neville, 16th Earl and infamous 'Kingmaker'.

Warwick's Great Fire of 1694 destroyed many of the central streets. The buildings torched (and many that were not) were rebuilt in the elegant style of the late 17th and early 18th centuries. St Mary's Church, which dominates the nearby countryside, received a new nave and tower at the same time. Several buildings survived the fire and can still be seen today, including the town's medieval Guildhall, now the Lord Leycester Hospital, and a cluster of timber-framed buildings around Oken's House.

Warwick Castle

Jephson Gardens, Leamington

Leamington Spa

A small village known as Leamington Priors until around 1800. The importance of the spa's mineral springs was recognised as early as the Middle Ages, but it wasn't until 1784 that the small hamlet began rediscovering its saline springs and building baths around them. C.S. Smith designed and built the Royal Pump Room and Baths, which opened in July 1814 at a cost of £30,000. 'Tendon stiffness, joint rigidity, the effects of gout and rheumatism, and various paralytic conditions' were all claimed to be cured or relieved by the spa treatment. The 'Royal Pump Room and Baths' made a lot of money in the beginning, but by 1848, the trend of 'taking the waters' had faded. Hard times loomed. Since then, the local council has done a lot to turn the pump rooms into a must-see location.

Kenilworth Castle

Kenilworth Castle [EH]

Castle Rd, Kenilworth, Warks CV8 1NG
www.english-heritage.org.uk

Built in the 1120s and served as a royal castle for most of its history. Although the castle's fortifications were demolished in 1650, many of the buildings have remained largely unchanged since Elizabeth I's reign. Simon de Montfort held Kenilworth against the king for six months in 1266, the longest siege in English medieval history.

In the 14th century, King Edward III's son, John of Gaunt, transformed the castle into a palace, constructing the great hall and lavish apartments. In the later Middle Ages, the castle was a favourite residence of the Lancastrian kings; Henry V even built a retreat at the far end of the lake.

Elizabeth I gave the castle to Robert Dudley, Earl of Leicester, in 1563, and he transformed it into a magnificent palace. In 1575, he famously entertained the queen here for 19 days of festivities.

Following the English Civil War, the castle's fortifications were demolished in 1650. Later, the ruins gained notoriety as a result of Walter Scott's 1821 novel Kenilworth, which romanticised the story of Robert Dudley, his wife Amy Robsart who died mysteriously after a fall down some stairs, and Elizabeth.

Grand Union Canal

Crosses by Warwickshire Event Ctr, CV31 1XN

Warwick and Birmingham Canal is a narrow canal which became part of the Grand Union Canal and runs under the Fosse.

Wappenbury Wood Nature Reserve

Burnthurst Ln, Princethorpe, Warks CV23 9QA
www.warwickshirewildlifetrust.org.uk

Richard of Wappenbury, mentioned in the Domesday Book, was granted limited rights over the woods. By the end of the 1400s, the wood provided the locals with fuel, building materials, and hunting opportunities. After being nearly felled twice in the 1940s and 1950s, the wood was left to regenerate naturally. The network of grassy rides and glades, provide peaceful walks through a wildlife haven. 88 bird species have been recorded, with frequent sightings of warblers, woodpeckers, and tawny owls.

Midland Air Museum

Baginton, Warks CV3 4FR
www.midlandairmuseum.co.uk

On May 15, 1941, the first British jet-powered plane took off from RAF Cranwell in Lincolnshire on a historic 17-minute flight. The jet age had begun! The story of Whittle's jet engine is told through photographs, video, and artefacts, including an animated display. The museum houses aircraft, engines, and supporting exhibits that tell the fascinating story of the jet age.

Bretford

The Fosse Way's original route was shifted westward in the Middle Ages to its current crossing point. The village's name is derived from the Old English bred ford, which means 'the plank ford' and was first recorded around 1100. Bretford was much more important in the Middle Ages than it is today. The lord of the manor, John de Verdon, founded it as a planned market town in 1227. It was also home to a leper hospital. Bretford declined after the Black Death in the 14th century and never recovered. During WWII, a lighting decoy site was established about 1km north-west of Bretford, with the goal of fooling German bombers into dropping their bombs harmlessly onto fields in the wrong location, rather than on their intended target of nearby Coventry.

Brinklow

There are remains of a large Norman motte-and-bailey castle, known locally as The Tump. The 13th century church is dedicated to St John the Baptist.

Stretton-under-Fosse

Along its main street, are several pretty cottages. An old manor house, Newbold Revel, just outside Stretton, was purchased in 1911 by RNID founder, a deaf banker and philanthropist, Leo Bonn. During the

nk hittle, inventor of the jet engine

First World War, Bonn donated Newbold Revel to be used as a military hospital.

High Cross

VERONIS

Now part of the A5, it was an important crossroads with Watling Street, known as Venonis. Satellite images show the remains of a fort and a settlement beneath the surface of a field to the south east of the crossroads. It is unknown how far it extended along the Fosse. Digs on the south side of Watling Street revealed timber building post holes, gullies, and slots. There was no complete building plan discovered. Hearths, pits, and gravel yard surfaces were unearthed. In 1722, the High Cross stone monument was built, funded by the Earl of Denbigh. It commemorated the Duke of Blenheim's victories against France as well as marking the centre of Roman Britain. It was made up of four Doric columns with an orb and cross above. Only the plinth remains today after a lightning strike in 1791. A wooden cross preceded the stone monument, which was the site of a medieval gibbet, a gallows-style structure where criminals' dead or dying bodies were publicly displayed to deter other current or would-be criminals. The gibbet itself was occasionally used as a method of execution, with the criminal left to die of exposure, thirst, or starvation.

Leicester Park and Ride

(South) St Johns, Enderby LE19 2AB
(West) Meynell's Gorse, Ratby Ln, LE3 3LF
(North) Birstall, Loughborough Rd, LE4 4NP

www.leicester.gov.uk

A quick and convenient route into the city centre.

Fosse Meadows Country Park

Roman Rd, Hinckley LE10 3AB
www.blaby.gov.uk

The park has extensive paths that wind through flower meadows, woodlands, and an arboretum. With a wildlife lake, bird hides, and a riverside walk that leads to a pond, it's a great place for bird watching.

National Gas Museum Trust

195 Aylestone Rd, Leicester LE2 7QH
www.nationalgasmuseum.org.uk

This compact museum depicts over 200 years of history, from the extraction of gas from coal to the lighting of Victorian London's streets. View a nostalgic collection of cookers, fires, and even a gas radio. Discover how natural gas became popular in homes and factories, as well as what the future holds.

Aylestone Meadows Local Nature Reserve

Leicester, LE2 8DZ
www.leicester.gov.uk

The meadows are home to a variety of wildlife and is Leicester's largest nature reserve. The Great Central Way forms part of Sustrans national cycle route 6. This four-mile pathway is ideal for walkers, and cyclists. Partly tarmacked, the level surface is ideal for those who have mobility restrictions or young cyclists gaining confidence. Many other pathways lead off around other areas of Aylestone including the canal towpath and boardwalks.

Medieval house in Leicester

Leicester

RATAE CORITANORUM

By 47 AD, the Romans had captured Leicestershire. In 48, they constructed a fort. The streets were laid out in a grid pattern, the centre reserved for a forum. Leicester was most likely abandoned after the Romans left. There may have been some people who lived within the walls and farmed the land outside, but it was no longer a town. However, in the late 7th century, town life in England began to revive. Leicester received a bishop and was a thriving town again by the 9th century. The main industry in medieval Leicester was wool. Leather and hosiery were also important. Pumps from public wells were installed in 1759, and the Royal Infirmary opened in 1771.

The city shot to fame in September 2012, when the skeletal remains of Plantagenet King Richard III, the last British monarch killed in battle, were discovered in a car park near the former Grey Friars Priory.

King Richard III Visitor Centre

4A St. Martins, Leicester, LE1 5DB
kriii.com

Visit the exact location where Richard III remained undiscovered for so long. Explore the incredible tale of the last English king to die in battle and the first to have his DNA tested. Discover the plot lines, birth rights, and family connections that came together to form an intricate plot of medieval murder, mystery, and mayhem.

Feel the cry of soldiers and the roar of hooves as the Plantagenets and Tudors collide, and where the king is killed as he defends his throne. Fast forward 500 years to a car park in Leicester city centre, where the incredible analysis that led to the discovery of King Richard III's long-lost remains is revealed. Be inspired by the science that identified the long-lost king.

Newarke Houses Museum

The Newarke, Leicester LE2 7BY
www.leicestermuseums.org

Explore more about Leicester's famous son Daniel Lambert, who became known as Britain's largest man. Visit a 1950s street scene based on Wharf Street, complete with the Jolly Angler public house, a grocer, and a pawnbroker, complete with sounds and conversations from the era. Learn about the home front and the history of the Leicestershire regiment through personal stories, including a recreation of a First World War trench.

Jewry Wall Museum [EH]

St Nicholas Circle, Leicester LE1 4LB
www.english-heritage.org.uk

This is one of the largest remaining Roman masonry structures in Britain. It was constructed around the year AD160 and served as the entrance to the public baths. The wall was later converted into the west wall of the original Saxon church of St Nicholas, ensuring its survival.

Leicester Cathedral

7 Peacock Lane, Leicester LE1 5PZ
leicestercathedral.org

St Martin's church was designated as a cathedral in 1927. It appears in the Domesday Book as one of six churches in Leicester. The church was rebuilt and expanded in the 13th century, and again in the 15th when the nave and aisles were extended. During the medieval period, St Martin's was used as the civic church by the guilds, who ran their affairs from the timber-framed guildhall next to the west end.

The connection to Richard III draws most visitors to Leicester Cathedral. His body was reinterred in front of millions of television viewers worldwide in 2015.

Temple Of Mithras Site

St Nicholas Circle, Leicester LE1 5LX
www.storyofleicester.info

A mithraeum was a place of worship for the Persian god. It was a popular mystery cult within the Roman empire. The temple was built in the early second century AD. Coins discovered on its final floor indicate that it was still in use in the late fourth. The temple was discovered south of the Jewry Wall in 1969 during the construction of a hotel on St Nicholas Circle.

Haymarket And Highcross Shopping Centres

Haymarket, 1 Kildare Walk LE1 3YH
Highcross, 5 Shires Lane LE1 4AN

Need a break from history? take a stroll round these modern shopping centres.

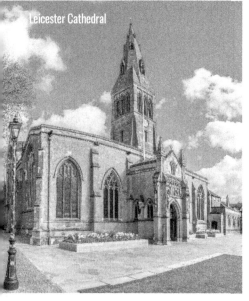
Leicester Cathedral

St Martins Square

St Martins Square, Leicester LE1 5DG
www.stmartinssquare.co.uk

St Martin's Square is a lovely place to spend an afternoon. The charming courtyard is surrounded by one-of-a-kind independent shops, restaurants, and salons, making this tranquil area a great place to sit and enjoy a coffee with friends, pick up a quirky gift, or shop for a new outfit.

Leicester Market

Market Pl, Leicester LE1 5GG
www.leicestermarket.co.uk

Leicester's market has a long and illustrious 700 year history. The Market Place was first mentioned in 1298, and Queen Elizabeth I referred to it as the 'Saturday Shambles' in a charter. It grew rapidly. Selling animals in the bustling centre was unjustifiable by the late 1800s. A new cattle market opened on Welford Road in 1872. The sheep, horse, and swine markets were also relocated.

In the early 20th century, as the city's largest public space, it became a venue for gatherings and rallies. These were frequently led by suffragette Alice Hawkins and unemployment rights activist Amos Sheriff. These two played major roles in the 100-mile march to London in 1905, raising awareness of the plight of the unemployed. A paving stone has been placed in front of the Corn Exchange steps in Leicester to commemorate this historic event. To mark the centennial of the Representation of the People Act 1918, which granted the right to vote to all men and some women, a statue of Alice was unveiled in February 2018.

National Space Centre

Exploration Drive, Leicester LE4 5NS
spacecentre.co.uk

The award-winning National Space Centre is an out of this world experience for the whole family. Home to the UK's largest planetarium, the centre has six interactive galleries, the iconic Rocket Tower, and hosts events throughout the year.

A cyberman at the space centre

Leicester Abbey And Park

Abbey Park Rd, Leicester LE4 5AQ
www.visitleicester.info

This park, which follows the banks of the River Soar in the city's north, is a lovely green space for relaxing and admiring Leicester's riverside scenery. Abbey Park is perfectly situated near the city centre and is walkable.

Statue Of Thomas Cook

London Rd, Leicester LE2 2PP
www.storyofleicester.info

The Thomas Cook statue was unveiled on 14 January 1994 by his great-great- grandson, also called Thomas. A cabinet-maker, he founded the Thomas Cook travel company in 1841 to carry temperance supporters by railway between Leicester, Nottingham, Derby and Birmingham. In 1851, Cook arranged transport to the Great Exhibition in London's Hyde Park. Four years later he organised trips to Europe and to the United States in 1866. He is buried, with other notable Leicester figures in Welford Road Cemetery.

Abbey Pumping Station Museum

Corporation Road, Leicester, LE4 5PX
www.abbeypumpingstation.org

Abbey Pumping Station is Leicester's Industrial Museum, showcasing the city's diverse industrial, technological, and scientific history. It tells the story of over 200 years of science and technology, from the early days of steam and industry to modern space exploration.

University Of Leicester Botanical Gardens

University Road, Leicester, LE1 7RH
le.ac.uk/botanic-garden

The gardens span 16 acres of lovingly cultivated grounds and greenhouses. See the alpine, tropical, temperate and cactus house environments.

The pond at the botanical gardens, NotFromUtrecht Wiki Commons

STAGE 5

LEICESTER TO LINCOLN

56 Miles

Explore the fens and expansive views of Lincolnshire. #

THE ROUTE

EXETER TO LINCOLN

- 🦶 0m Leicester
- 🦶 14m Six Hills (A607/A46)
- 🦶 13m Saxondale (A46)
- 🦶 12m Newark-upon-Trent (A46)
- 🦶 17m Lincoln (A46)

LINCOLN TO EXETER

- 🦶 0m Lincoln
- 🦶 17m Newark-upon-Trent (A46)
- 🦶 12m Saxondale (A46)
- 🦶 13m Six Hills (A46)
- 🦶 14m Leicester (A607)

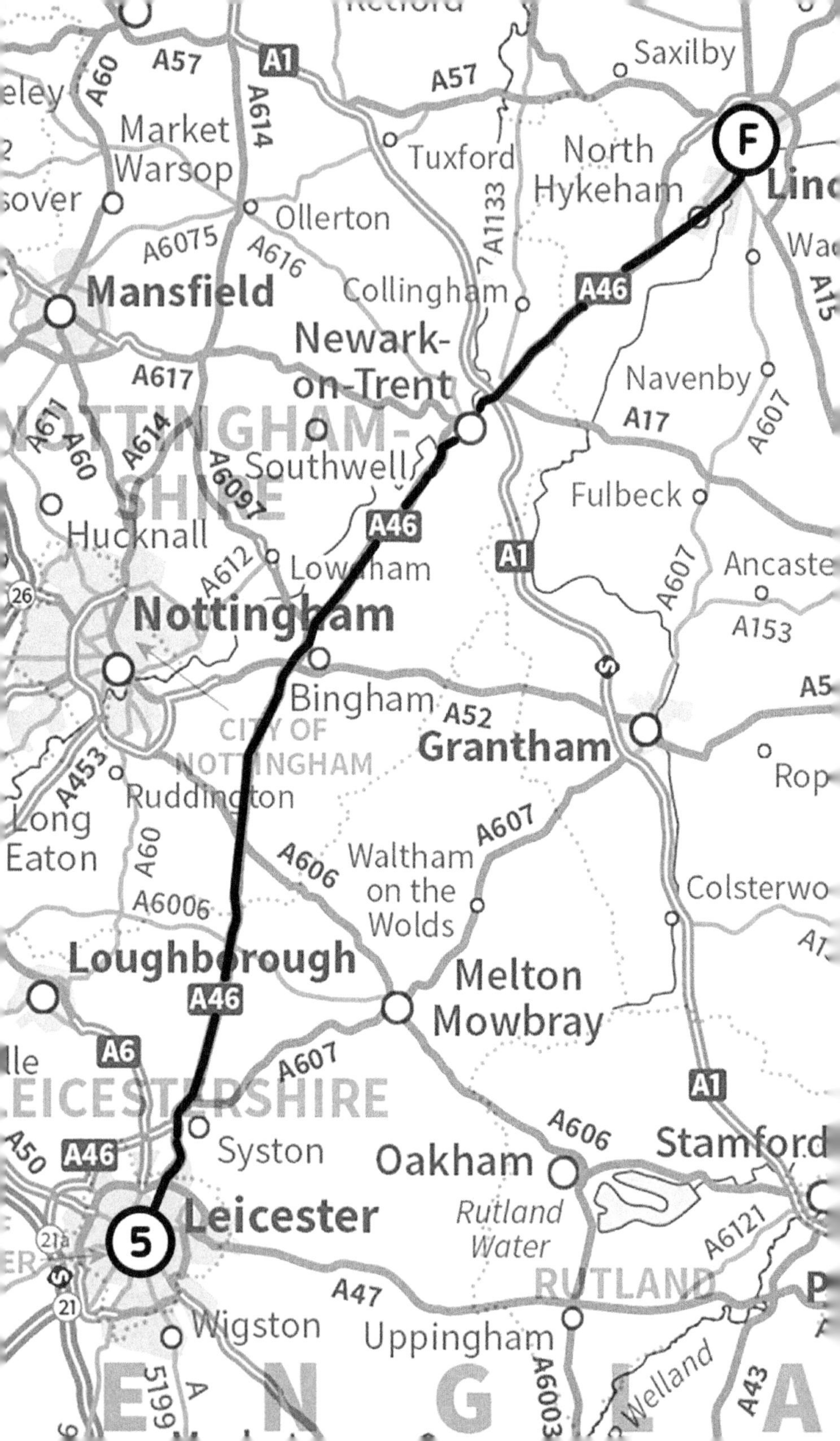
Saxilby
A57
A1
A60
Market
Warsop
A614
Tuxford
North
Hykeham
Ollerton
A1133
A6075
A616
Mansfield
Collingham
A46
Newark-
on-Trent
Navenby
A617
A17
A607
NOTTINGHAM-
SHIRE
Southwell
Fulbeck
A6097
A611
A60
A614
Hucknall
A1
Ancaste
A612
Lowdham
A153
Nottingham
Bingham
A52
Grantham
CITY OF
NOTTINGHAM
A453
Ruddington
Long
Eaton
A607
A606
Waltham
on the
Wolds
Colsterwo
A6006
Loughborough
Melton
Mowbray
A6
A607
LEICESTERSHIRE
A1
A606
Syston
Stamford
A50
Oakham
Leicester
Rutland
Water
A6121
RUTLAND
A47
Wigston
Uppingham
A6003
Welland
A43
ENGLA
5
F

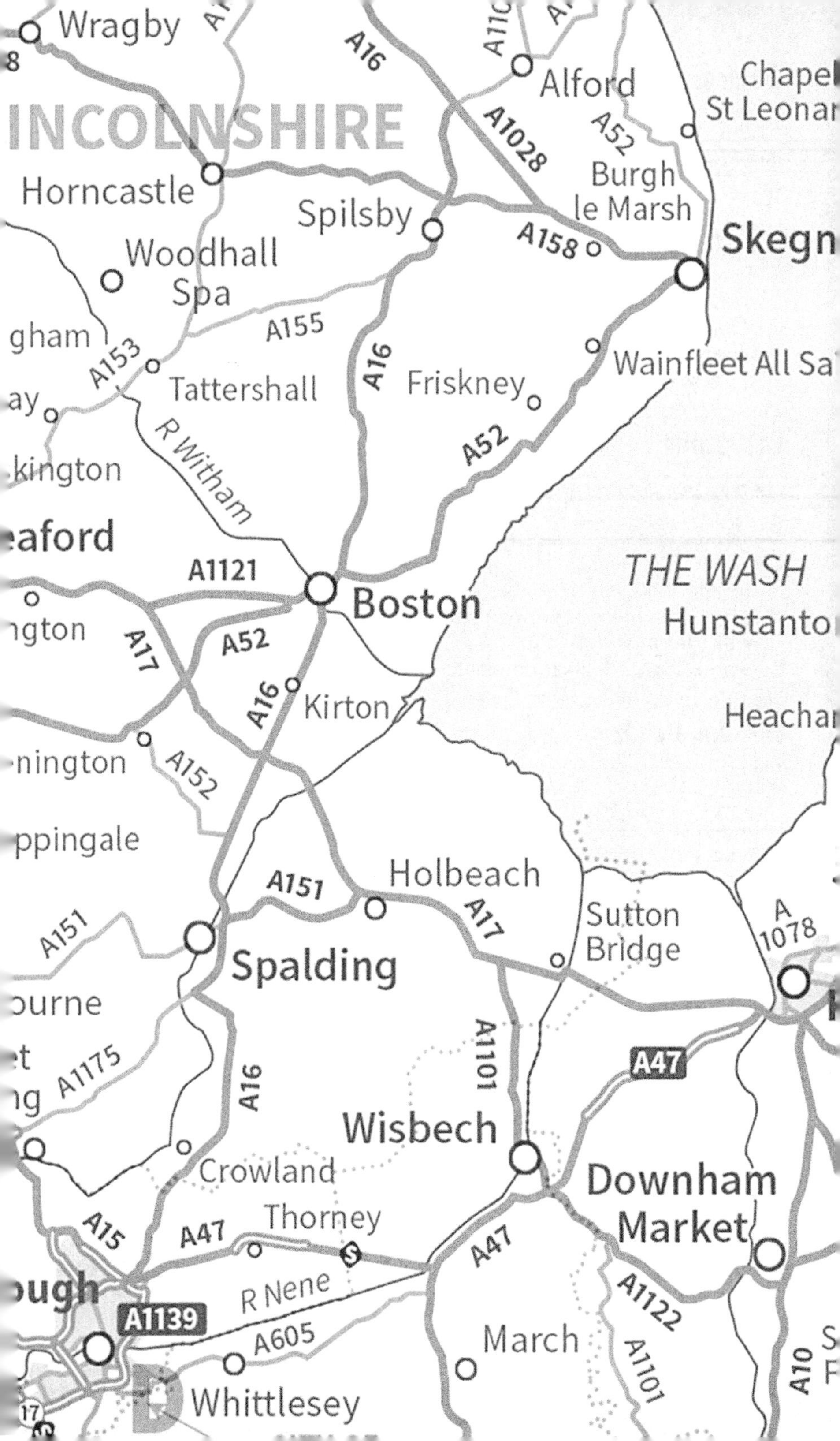

Wragby

A16

A110

A16

Alford

Chapel
St Leonar

LINCOLNSHIRE

A1028

A52

Burgh
le Marsh

Horncastle

Spilsby

A158

Skegn

Woodhall
Spa

A153

Wainfleet All Sa

gham

Tattershall

A155

A16

Friskney

ay

R Witham

A52

kington

eaford

A1121

THE WASH

ngton

A17

A52

Boston

Hunstanto

A16

Kirton

Heacha

nington

A152

ppingale

A151

Holbeach

A17

Sutton
Bridge

A
1078

A151

Spalding

ourne

A1175

A16

A1101

A47

t

ng

Wisbech

Downham
Market

Crowland

A15

A47

Thorney

A47

A1122

A10

ough

A1139

R Nene

A605

March

A1101

Whittlesey

Watermead Nature Reserve

Wanlip Rd, Fillingate, Leics, LE7 8PF
www.leicscountryparks.org.uk

This is one of the best places in Leicestershire for bird watching and nature walks. Since the early 1980s, this area has been designated as a reserve. The park's surfaced paths are ideal for walking, running, and cycling, and many benches along these trails are ideal places to sit and relax.

East Stoke

East Stoke, Newark NG23 5QL
www.nottinghamshire.gov.uk

The Battle of Stoke Field took place on 16 June 1487, the last battle of the infamous Wars of the Roses, two years after Richard III was slain at Bosworth, close to Market Bosworth.

Farndon Ponds

Wyke Ln, Farndon, Newark NG24 3TH
www.newark-sherwooddc.gov.uk

Farndon Ponds Nature Reserve is a large pond located between the village of Farndon and the Trent River, a favourite spot for dog walkers, joggers, and families. The area is ideal for bird watching, walking, and admiring the local wildlife. Farndon Marina is good for some boat spotting. Although you can't access the private marina, there is a good vantage point from the nearby bridge.

Cotgrave Country Park

Hollygate Ln, Nottingham NG12 3HE
cotgravecountrypark.co.uk

200 acres of open space to explore. The Grantham Canal is close by too.

Newark-Upon-Trent

Newark is located on the Trent, the A1, the historic Great North Road, and the East Coast Main Line railway. Because of its location on the Fosse Way, the town's origins are possibly Roman.

An Anglo-Saxon pagan cemetery, dating from the early 5th to early 7th centuries, has been discovered near the Fosse Way and the Trent in Millgate.

During Edward the Confessor's reign, Newark belonged to Godiva and her husband Leofric, Earl of Mercia. King Edward the Elder founded Newark Castle as a Saxon fortified manor house. Remigius de Fécamp, Bishop of Lincoln, established an earthwork motte-and-bailey fortress on the site in 1073. The river bridge, as well as St Leonard's Hospital, were built around this time under a charter from Henry I. King John died of dysentery in the castle after 'gorging on a surfeit of (too many) of peaches'.

Henry VIII executed the Vicar of Newark, Henry Lytherland, for refusing to recognise the king as the head of the Church. During the civil war, Newark was an important Royalist stronghold, with Charles I raising his standard in nearby Nottingham. In 1645, Newark cavalry fought alongside the king's forces, who were soundly defeated at the Battle of Naseby, also near Leicester.

River Trent

The third-longest river in the UK. Its source is in Staffordshire and it flows into the River Humber. It is still an important waterway carrying a significant amount of commercial traffic, particularly in its lower reaches. It is tidal below Cromwell Lock and is subject to a periodic tidal bore similar to that seen on the River Severn.

Newark Castle

Newark Waterfalls

11 Coopers Yard, Newark NG24 4UH

At Newark, the Trent River splits into several smaller channels, all of which eventually recombine with the main river. The Trent Waterfalls are a series of weirs on one of the smaller branches that splits off from the main river. A photogenic location, with many trees lining the banks.

National Civil War Museum

14 Appletongate, Newark NG24 1JY
www.nationalcivilwarcentre.com

Plunge into the midst of Britain's deadliest dispute. Learn about gunpowder, plague, and plots from this dramatic period in British history. Discover the clashes between Roundhead and Royalist, brother and brother, and how a once all-powerful king succumbed to the axeman. Discover the causes, conflicts, and consequences of the war through expertly curated objects and analysis,

as well as a fascinating look at life in a town that was besieged three times between 1643 and 1646.

Newark Air Museum

Drove Lane, Newark, Notts NG24 2NY
www.newarkairmuseum.org

On the site of the former World War II airfield of Winthorpe, it exhibits a collection of over 90 aircraft and cockpit sections, spanning the entire history of aviation. With extensive under cover displays, including two halls with over 48 aircraft and helicopters, there is something to see or do whatever the weather.

Town Hall Museum

Market Pl, Newark, Notts NG24 1DU
www.newarktownhallmuseum.co.uk

This is one of the country's finest Georgian town halls. The eminent architect John Carr of York designed it in the Palladian style in 1774. The museum includes rooms within the working town hall that house a fine collection of civic treasures. Original Georgian features can be found in the imposing Council Chamber, the Mayor's Parlour, and an elegant Assembly Room that was restored to its 18th century splendour in 1990.

Brough

Brough stands on the site of the Roman town of Crococalana, which grew around a military fort in the 1st century AD. The town spread along the Fosse Way for about a mile, and had ditched defences.

Doddington Hall And Gardens

Doddington, Lincoln, Lincs LN6 4RU
www.doddingtonhall.com

Begun in 1595 by Robert Smythson, one of England's foremost Elizabethan architects, Doddington Hall was completed in 1600. It is a now privately owned home open to the public, surrounded by stunning gardens.

Bomber Command Centre

Canwick Avenue, Lincoln, Lincs LN4 2HQ
internationalbcc.co.uk

The museum looks at the efforts, sacrifices, and commitment of the men and women from 62 different countries who served in Bomber Command during WWII. The project also tells the stories of those who suffered as a result of the bombing campaigns and those whose survival was ensured by Bomber Command's humanitarian operations. Despite suffering the highest losses of any unit during WWII, Bomber Command has struggled for recognition. It was a volunteer aircrew, and sadly, the average life expectancy was just 23.

The Natural World at Whisby Nature Park

Moor Ln, Thorpe-on-the-Hill, Lincs LN6 9BW
www.naturalworldcentre.org

A large reserve known for its ponds and lakes, with over six miles of footpaths suitable for buggies and mobility scooters. It encompasses 150 hectares of natural habitat, including a complex of small, medium, and large flooded gravel pits that have been reclaimed by 40 years of natural colonisation. It has a diverse bird population that can be seen from several strategically placed hides. The park has six well-marked trails ranging in length from 1.2 to 3 miles.

The walks are level and have a hard surface of compacted limestone in many places.

Doddington Hall

Lincoln Cathedral

Lincoln

LINDON

Lincoln's first known settlement, dating back to the 1ˢᵗ century BC, was around the Brayford Waterfront area, giving the city its original name Lindon. The Romans settled around AD 50, and built a wooden fortress at the top of the hill, which was later converted into a colonia, a retirement home for soldiers. Ermine Street, another key Roman highway connecting London and York, ran through Lincoln. In the 9ᵗʰ and 10ᵗʰ centuries, Vikings ruled Lincoln, and the settlement grew into a small trading town. Street and place names like Bailgate, Danesgate, Wragby, and Skellingthorpe have ties to this era. In 1068, William the Conqueror led the Norman invasion of the city, ordering the construction of Lincoln Castle and, later, Lincoln Cathedral on the site of the former Roman settlement. When the spire on the central tower of

Lincoln Cathedral was raised in 1300, it surpassed the Great Pyramid as the tallest building in the world. It held that title until it collapsed during a storm in 1549.

Ellis' Mill

Mill Road, Lincoln LN1 3LY
www.visitlincoln.com

Built in 1798, it was the last of nine windmills that once stood on the Lincoln hilltop and the last working mill in Lincoln. It is the sole survivor of its type and a fine example of a small tower mill.

Boultham Park

55 Hall Dr, Lincoln LN6 7SW
http://www.boulthampark.co.uk

A 50-acre park with greens, woodlands, a lake, and a children's playground. In the 18ᵗʰ and 19ᵗʰ centuries, it was part of a manorial estate. During World War I it served as a convalescence home and as part of the 'Dig for Victory' campaign during World War II. The council purchased the parkland and it opened in 1930.

Lincoln Cathedral

Minster Yard, Lincoln LN2 1PX
lincolncathedral.com

Described by Victorian writer John Ruskin 'as out and out the most precious piece of architecture in the British Isles and roughly speaking worth any two other cathedrals we have', it is not to be missed. Despite its size, the cathedral is densely packed with intricate detail. The architects of the Gothic style may have reached the pinnacle of their craft in Lincoln Cathedral; it is an absolute must-see for anyone visiting Lincoln.

Museum of Lincolnshire Life

Burton Road, Lincoln LN1 3LY
www.lincolnshire.gov.uk

The rich and diverse social history collection at the museum reflects and celebrates the culture of Lincolnshire and its people from 1750 to the present. Exhibits depict various aspects of commercial, domestic, agricultural, industrial, and community life. The museum houses an authentic World War One tank named 'Daphne,' as well as interactive galleries of the Royal Lincolnshire Regiment that have won prestigious national awards.

Brayford Waterfront

Brayford Wharf, Lincoln LN1 1X

England's oldest inland harbour, offering a great selection of eating, drinking and entertainment venues.

Lincoln Castle

Castle Square, Lincoln LN1 3AA
www.lincolncastle.com

Built by William the Conqueror in 1068, the castle has stood for hundreds of years as a symbol of power and the seat of justice. Explore 1,000 years of history—right where it happened. Scale the medieval wall walk, stroll in the Footsteps of Victorian Prison inmates, and be immersed in the Magna Carta story.

Lincoln Castle

Medieval Bishops' Palace [EH]

Minster Yard, Lincoln LN2 1PU
www.english-heritage.org.uk

The medieval bishops' palace was once one of the most important buildings in the country, standing almost in the shadow of Lincoln Cathedral and offering sweeping views of the ancient city and the countryside beyond. Its architecture reflects enormous power and wealth. Be guided by the audio tour as you visit the undercrofted East Hall, the chapel range and the entrance tower built by Bishop William Alnwick, who modernised the palace in the 1430s. Take a moment to relax and enjoy the Heritage Garden, a peaceful and tranquil haven.

The Collection Museum and Art Gallery

Danes Terr, Lincoln, LN2 1LP
www.thecollectionmuseum.com

Award-winning archaeology museum located in the heart of historic Lincoln, with interactive exhibitions, events and talks, and guided tours.

Lincoln Arboretum

Monks Road, Lincoln, LN5 7AY
www.lincoln.gov.uk

The arboretum is a historic park with a grade II designation. Between 1870 and 1872, it was designed and laid out by Edward Milner, one of the most celebrated Victorian gardeners of his time. Enjoy the beautiful gardens, lakes, fountains, and bridges, as well as the Victorian bandstand and children's play area in this well-maintained park.

Steep Hill

Steep Hill, Lincoln, LN2 1LU
www.visitlincoln.com

Steep Hill, built by the Romans and originally with steps, connects Lincoln's historic Cathedral Quarter to the more modern city centre. Those who are brave enough to walk up the hill are rewarded with independent boutique stores, tea rooms, historic pubs, and spectacular views of the city and countryside, as well as access to the castle and cathedral. The ascent definitely gets the blood pumping. According to the Ordnance Survey team, Steep Hill officially has the fourth steepest average incline in England, at 16.12°. For those preferring a more leisurely ascent, the Walk and Ride service (also known as the 'Steep Hill Shuttle' or the 'Castle Shuttle') takes passengers directly to the Cathedral Quarter without having to negotiate Steep Hill.

Jew's House

15 The Strait, Lincoln, LN2 1JD
www.visitlincoln.com

The Jew's House

One of England's oldest and most important domestic dwellings. It is situated on Steep Hill, below the Jew's Court. The house has long been associated with medieval Lincoln's thriving Jewish community. It was last owned by Belaset, daughter of Solomon of Wallingford, before the Jews were expelled from England in 1290. The magnificence of the entry, its off-centre location, and the absence of an original front entrance to Jew's Court next door all point to it being the original entrance to the medieval synagogue thought to be behind the court. The house is one of only five surviving Medieval Jewish houses in England, a testament to Lincoln's prominent Jewish community in the 12th and 13th centuries.

Newport Arch

Bailgate, Lincoln LN1 3DQ
www.visitlincoln.com

One of the surviving jewels of Roman Britain. When Lindum Colonia, became the capital of Flavia Caesariensis in the 4th century, the arch was remodelled and enlarged. It is unique in Britain as it is the only original Roman arch still open to traffic. It served as the city's north gate, carrying the major Roman road, Ermine Street, northward almost in a straight line to the Humber. It has been hit by lorries three times—but has survived.

Temple Gardens

Lindum Road, Lincoln LN2 1NP
www.visitlincoln.com

In the early 19th century, Joseph Moore established the area, originally part of the lower city's Roman defences, as a garden and displayed local artwork to paying visitors. The 1861 Lincoln Exhibition, for example, drew 30,000 people. In 1927, the then-Prince of Wales reopened it as a public space, along with the Sir Reginald Blomfield-designed Usher Gallery.

Greetwell Hollow Nature Reserve

Nearest postcode LN2 4HY
www.lincstrust.org.uk

The valley's limestone grassland supports a diverse range of wildflowers, including bee orchids, and the scrub provides excellent habitat for wintering and nesting birds. The stream that runs through the reserve's heart supports wetlands and attracts wintering snipe, moorhen, and heron.

What3Words: ///corn.folds.itself

ROMAN FOOD AND DRINK

Food from the Empire

Roman food was simple and similar to ancient Greek food. Cereals, peas, beans and lentils, vegetables, fruits, meat, fish, and shellfish were popular as well as olive oil, vinegar, salt, pepper, mint, saffron, and other spices. A popular breakfast called *puls* was made of a wheat-related grain called emmer, olive oil, salt, and various herbs.

Roman cuisine's evolution

Rome's expansion of the republic and empire, encouraged the adoption of foreign culinary habits. As it grew, the disparities in eating habits between social classes became more pronounced. Roman cuisine became more refined.

Although eating three times a day was introduced by the Romans, it was only practised by the wealthy. Most people in the ancient world only ate once.

Breakfast, *jentaculum*, was light, typically consisting of a piece of bread dipped in honey or cheese. Lunch, *cena*, was a substantial meal and the main meal of the day. Dinner, *verspersena*, was a light supper.

Cena became more important and was eaten later, evolving into a three-course meal by the end of the Republic: the appetiser, *gustatio*, the main course, *primae mensae*, and the dessert, *secundae mensae*.

Social class and eating habits

The eating habits of ordinary Romans differed greatly from those of the upper class. Ordinary Romans (and slaves) ate less frequently, and were standing up or sitting around a table, whereas wealthy Romans ate reclined on couches in the triclinium, a luxurious room. Commoners couldn't afford even the oil lamps required to illuminate them at night. Plus, commoners had to get up early the next morning to get to work, so they went to bed early rather than eating a heavy meal late in the day. Dining was a lavish and entertaining culinary experience for the upper class, but it was a necessity for most citizens.

The average Roman could not afford to eat meat and all the exotic foods from the provinces that their rich brethren did.

Flavours of the empire

Roman cuisine was often sweet and sour, similar to Asian cuisines today. They enjoyed adding sweet fruits and honey and a tart taste from vinegar to dishes.

Bread. Bread was a staple consumed by all social classes. Over 30 bakeries and many rotary mills to grind grain were discovered in Pompeii, proving that Romans ate a lot of it! Bread was frequently eaten with honey, olives, eggs, cheese, or moretum, a cheese, garlic, and herb spread. (A recipe from a Roman farmer, Columella, has been included in this book.) They often sprayed salt on their bread and dipped it in wine, considering it perfectly normal. Bread was originally made of emmer but later Romans began making bread with wheat, just like today.

However, their tasted very different from nowadays. The bread flour was not as pure as the flour used today. It frequently contained a lot of dust and bits which made the bread coarse, so coarse that people's teeth wore down over time as they chewed on it!

Legumes, vegetables, and fruits. Nutritious beans, peas, and lentils were cooked by the ancient Romans.

They also ate a lot of raw and cooked vegetables and fruits. Many of them associated with Mediterranean cuisine today, however, did not exist in ancient Rome. Tomatoes, potatoes, and capsicum peppers, popular in Italy today, for example, were introduced to Europe only after the discovery of the New World in the 1400s. The Arabs introduced aubergine between 600 and 700 AD. Fruits such as lemons and oranges were uncommon until the time of the end of the empire.

What they did have was cabbage, celery, kale, broccoli, radishes, asparagus, yellow squash, carrots, turnips, beets, peas, and cucumber, plus apples, figs, grapes, pears, and olives. For carrots, the Romans had a variety of colours, not just orange, now sadly extinct.

Meat and fish. Fish and seafood were typically more common and less expensive than meat, which was considered a luxury. The Romans cooked fish, sardines, tuna, sea bass, shellfish, and seafood like octopus. There were many large fisheries in Rome. Aquaculture, including fish and oyster farming, was a highly developed industry. Poultry like chicken and game were popular. Romans ate salted pork and lamb, with beef being less common.

The rich also consumed rodents such as dormice, which were regarded as a delicacy and a status symbol. The well-to-do would weigh the rodents in front of their guests before cooking to show off their wealth.

Garum. This was a fermented fish sauce and was a staple of Roman cuisine, used in a variety of dishes, and as a table condiment. It was created by fermenting the intestines of small fish.

Drinks. Many drinks that are commonly consumed today did not exist in ancient Rome. Coffee, originally an Arab drink, yet often associated with Italy, did not exist. It arrived in the 1500s. Coffee was dubbed 'the Muslim drink' in Europe for a long time before Pope Clement VIII declared it Christian in 1600.

Tea, an Asian drink introduced to Europe by the Dutch in the 17th century, did not exist in ancient Rome either.

Romans preferred alcoholic beverages to water, despite having access to relatively high quality water via the aqueducts. Alcoholic beverages were thought to be safer to drink and tastier. The Romans drank mostly wine, although not in the same way we do today. Their wine had a higher alcohol content and was watered down before consumption. Some historians say it was considered 'barbaric' to consume undiluted wine. The Romans also added spices and even honey to their wine, which was frequently served hot. It was stored in clay pots called amphoras rather than glass bottles.

The plebeians and the army drank posca, an alcoholic beverage despised by the upper class. Posca was made from acetum, a cheap wine that tasted almost like vinegar. Spoiled, vinegary wine would also be used to make this ancient Roman beverage. Diluted acetum was mixed with various herbs and spices, usually crushed coriander seeds. Honey was frequently used to sweeten it.

Beer, cerevisiae, and honey mead were more popular in the Northern provinces. Many Romans considered beer drinking to be barbaric, as it was frequently associated with 'barbarians', namely the Gauls and the Huns.

Milk was also frowned upon as a drink and was only to be used in cheese production.

MAKE A ROMAN RECIPE

Moretun

Columella's Fresh Cheese and Herb Dip 'Moretum'

This dish was a simple, vegetarian meal made with cheese, herbs and other greens, and condiments like olive oil or vinegar. It gets its name from a common kitchen implement found throughout the classical Mediterranean: the mortarium. The author of this recipe, Lucius Columella (4 BC-70 AD) was a respected farmer who described early Roman-era food and farming in his writings entitled De Re Rustica (65 AD).

Equipment

☐ A knife for chopping
☐ A spoon or fork for mashing
☐ A bowl

Ingredients

☐ 450 gr of fresh ricotta cheese
☐ ½ tsp dried mint or 10 fresh leaves
☐ ½ tsp coriander or 10 fresh
☐ 1 tsp dried or a sprig of fresh leaves
☐ A handful of fresh parsley
☐ Chives or spring onions to taste
☐ A handful of rocket
☐ Salt and fresh pepper to taste

Preparation

• Wash and chop your green ingredients.

• Put them in a bowl and crush them (using a spoon instead of a pestle) until you have a paste.

• Add the cheese, salt, and pepper to the bowl a bit at a time so you get the taste and texture you want.

• Transfer the moretum into a serving bowl and drizzle it with some olive oil.

• Serve with fresh-baked bread and enjoy!

REGIONAL FOOD AND DRINK

Devonshire Food

Sadly, the days of tucking into a Roman roast dormouse are long gone, but there are a host of modern delicacies to try as you explore the Fosse Way.

Devonshire Cream Tea

These have been made with cream on the bottom and jam on top since the 11th century, when the tradition of eating bread with cream and jam began at Tavistock Abbey in Devon. There is still a lot of fierce debate between the Devonians and Cornish on whether the cream or jam should go on first.

Devon Flats

Round biscuits made of wheat flour, clotted cream, sugar, and egg, lightly baked until golden.

Devonshire Junket

This chilled dessert is a West Country staple that makes the most of Devon's rich cream and milk. Traditionally served with clotted cream and soft fruit.

Devonshire Squab Pie

An old-style English pastry-topped pie made with lamb, apples, and onions, with no baby pigeons (aka squabs) in sight!

Exeter Pudding

A bread and sponge pudding laced with custard and apricot or blackcurrant jam.

Gingerbread

In the past, at West Country fairs, special sweetmeats, gingerbread, and spiced ale were traditionally served. The most well-known of these was Widecombe Fair, which took place on the 2nd Tuesday of September, in central Dartmoor.

Clotted Cream Fudge

Devonshire fudge

Fudge is not an ancient food. It probably originated in the States, with a widely accepted (though not undisputed) story from 1886. A New York student's failed attempts to make caramel earned the result the name of 'fudge'. The Devonians made it their own by adding—you guessed it—clotted cream.

Whitepot Rice Pudding

Whitepot, a decadent early Stuart dessert recipe from 1615, is particularly associated with Devon. These rice pudding 'whitepot' recipes were extremely popular in the 1600s.

Smoked Mackerel Pate

While the sleek silvery mackerel spend the winter in water around 300m deep, they return to the shallows off the coast in the summer months in shoals numbering the thousands, making them a popular catch for Devonshire fishermen.

Hog's Pudding

Hog's pudding

Hog's pudding is a two-inch-diameter sausage produced in parts of Devon and Cornwall. Some variations of the recipe call for pork meat and fat, suet, bread, and oatmeal or pearl barley shaped into the shape of a large sausage—also known as 'groats pudding.' It's spicy and flavourful, with black pepper, cumin, basil, and garlic added to the mixture.

Potted Crab

Every summer, crab is celebrated at South Devon Crab Month.

Devonshire Split

These are a variation on the cream tea. These are made from yeast dough and are split down the middle before being filled with clotted cream and jam.

Devonshire Drinks

Exeter Brewery

Avocet, County Best, Darkness, Fall's Over, Ferryman, Fraid Not, IPL It's Proper Lager, Lighterman, Sumasider, Tomahawk

Dartmoor Brewery

Jail Ale, Legend, Dartmoor IPA, Dartmoor Best, Dragon's Breath, Three Hares

Hanlon's Brewery

Yellow Hammer, Port Stout, Firefly Bitter, Stormstay Ale, Citra IPA,

Hanlons CBD, Chequered Flag , Grand Prix, Hill Climb, Prescott IOA, Crystal Clear Lager, Prescott Lager

Roaming Brew

Endless Summer, I'm a Good Swimmer, Hometown Pale, Helles Lager

Gloucestershire Food

Gloucester Old Spot

The Gloucestershire Old Spots are a hardy breed of pigs and live quite happily outside. Whilst they must have

Old Spot, Amanda Slater Flickr

one clear spot there are no set numbers of spots and people have mixed views on how many they like with some opting for lots of spots whilst others for very few.

Stinking Bishop

Charles Martell makes the cheese on his farm in the heart of Gloucestershire. It gets its name from the pear variety 'Stinking Bishop.' The juice is made into a perry and used to wash the cheese.

Single Gloucester

Single Gloucester is a lighter and younger cheese than Double Gloucester. It must be made in Gloucestershire and contain some milk from Old Gloucester cows. These cows are one of the oldest and most endangered breeds in the United Kingdom. There was only one herd left in Britain in 1972, but the breed is now thriving thanks to

cheesemaking. It was traditionally made by farmers' wives and kept on the farm for the family. Because it was not for sale, it was not coloured like the Double Gloucester, and it was consumed at a younger age. This resulted in a distinctive creamy mellowness.

Gloucestershire Beers

The New Flying Monk Brewery

Mighty Monk, Habit, Elmers

Corinian Ales

Corinium Gold, Centurion Stout, Ale Caesar IPA, Bodicacia Golden, Plautus Pale Ale, Firebird Red Ale, Pliny the Elderflower Pale Ale, 1 Ad Porter, Saturnalia

Leicestershire Food

Melton Mowbray Pork Pies

These must be made in the Melton Mowbray style and within a specific area surrounding Melton Mowbray. Hot water crust pastry is used to make these pies. Unlike other pork pies, they are not cooked in a case, which gives them their distinctive, gently bowed, sides. According to pie connoisseurs, not baking in a tin also contributes to the pastry's deep golden brown outer colour.

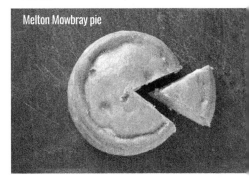
Melton Mowbray pie

Bosworth Jumbles

Bosworth Jumbles are simple S-shaped biscuits made with sugar, flour, butter, and eggs. They may have been a delight in the 15th century, but today only 3% of people have heard of them, and the biscuits are on the verge of extinction.

Pukka Pies

Trevor and Valerie Storer baked their first pies in 1963. The word of a good pie spreads quickly, and the couple sold over a thousand pies in their first week. The Storers' pie popularity grew quickly as they sold their signature Steak & Kidney pie to pubs, fish and chip shops and locals. They quickly devised new recipes to keep their satisfied customers coming back for more. In the UK and abroad, they now sell around 60 million pies per year.

Red Leicester Cheese

Originally coloured with carrot or beetroot juice, the cheese was made on farms in Leicestershire, England, with leftover milk after all of the Stilton desired was made. It was originally known as Leicestershire Cheese, but it was renamed Red Leicester to distinguish it from 'White Leicester,' which was made according to a national wartime recipe in the 1940s due to rationing.

Stilton

To use the name 'Stilton' cheese must be made in one of the three counties of Derbyshire, Leicestershire, or Nottinghamshire, and must use pasteurised local milk. Stilton was famous for cheese in 1724, according to Daniel Defoe's 'Tour through the Villages of England & Wales,' and the cheese was referred to as the 'English Parmesan.'

Leicestershire Drinks

Anstey Ale Brewery

Father's Favourite, Packhorse Bridge Best Bitter, Darkroom Oatmeal Stout, Paleface IPA.

Belvoir Brewery

Dark Horse, Whippling, Star Bitter, Gordon Bennett, Beaver Bitter, Old Dalby

Charnwood Brewery

Salvation, and Vixen

Dow Bridge Brewery

Bonum Mild, Acris, Centurion, Ratae'd, Dark, Gladiator.

Parish Brewery

Baz's Bonce Blower, PSB, Burrough Bitter, Poachers Ale

Pig Pub Brewery

Weiner Bitter, Pig Out, Claybrooke Bitter, Pig's Best Bitter

Lincolnshire Food

Haslet

A herb-infused pork meatloaf from Lincolnshire. Although the word haslet is derived from the Old French 'hastilles', which means entrails, haslet is typically made from stale white bread, minced pork, sage, salt, and black pepper. It's usually served cold, with pickles and salad, or as a sandwich filling.

Lincolnshire Sausages

Lincolnshire sausages

The herb sage is commonly dominant, rather than the more peppery flavour balance found in other regional English sausages such as the Cumberland. Other herbs, such as parsley and thyme, are frequently used, but these are not considered authentic Lincolnshire sausages. They are also distinguished by their open, chunky texture, which is the result of coarsely ground rather than minced pork.

Plum Loaf and Lincolnshire Poacher Cheese

Unlike the Lincolnshire Poacher Cheese, the Plum Loaf is made by several Lincolnshire bakers, each with their own unique twist on the original recipe. It was first made in 1901 by Charles Myers in the small market town of Alford in Lincolnshire. Dried fruit, and spices such as cinnamon, nutmeg and allspice give it its flavour.

Lincolnshire Poacher Cheese is a handcrafted, award-winning cheese made from raw cow's milk. The sole producer is Simon Jones of FW Read & Sons also in Alford. It's made on the family farm using old-fashioned methods. It takes between 12 and 24 months to develop the flavour as a slow maturing cheese. The flavour varies depending on the season, with a distinct taste that is slightly sweet and nutty. It is a hard cheese with a smooth texture that is described as a cross between West Country Cheddar and Gruyere.

Lincolnshire Drinks

Ferry Ales Brewery

Smokey Joe Porter, Witham Shield Pale Ale, 49 Squadron Best Bitter, Just Jane Bitter, Spirit of Jane Pale Bitter, Golden Fleece Blonde, Cossack Russian Imperial, Lincoln Lager, Harvest Gold, Mandarina East Coast IPA, Fabuccino Coffee Milk Stout, Mosquito English Pale Ale, Push The Envelope IPA, Lincoln Red Red Ale, Magic Ale, FIDO Best Bitter

Firehouse Brewery

Windy Landlady, FGB, Endeavour Gold, Mainwaring's Mild, Hump Lammer Stout, Wobbly Weasel, Lincolnshire Country Bitter

Harrison's Brewery

Vacant Gesture, Proof of Concept, Coconut Pale Ale, Leafs A Bitch, Weed Hatch, Mango Sorbet IPA, Raspberry WildBrew Sour

PACKING LIST

Someone packing (or is that repacking?)

Some handy prompts for things you might want to take with you on your trip. Over time, think about what you needed and didn't have with you and what you did have but didn't use to refine your list each time. Try to keep things in the same place so they're easy to find and store, else chaos reigns.

Power and Light

Check the batteries of these a few days before you go so there's time to charge them.

- ☐ Rechargeable batteries
- ☐ Rechargeable power packs
- ☐ Headtorch/torch batteries
- ☐ Camera battery
- ☐ Mattress air pump
- ☐ Car battery booster pack
- ☐ Jump leads
- ☐ Electronics cables/adapters
- ☐ Camper interior lights
- ☐ Power inverter
- ☐ Electric hook up lead

Essentials

Keep these handy...

- ☐ Money
- ☐ Wallet
- ☐ Credit card
- ☐ Phone/GPS

- ☐ Phone charger
- ☐ Camera
- ☐ Personal medication(s)
- ☐ Snacks
- ☐ Beverages
- ☐ Paper towels/napkins
- ☐ Plastic bags/sheets

Paper backups

In case there's no signal or your phone goes flat...

- ☐ Important phone numbers
- ☐ Booking confirmations
- ☐ Tickets
- ☐ Printed directions
- ☐ Maps and guides

Travel Comfort

- ☐ Hat
- ☐ Gloves
- ☐ Sunglasses
- ☐ Regular glasses
- ☐ Sweatshirt

Lastminute Packing

Get these close to your camp

- [ ] Cooler ice
- [ ] Cold/hot drinks
- [ ] Takeaway meal
- [ ] Fresh water
- [ ] Milk

Personal Hygiene

- [ ] Toothbrush and paste
- [ ] Floss
- [ ] Mouthwash
- [ ] Deodorant
- [ ] Hand sanitiser
- [ ] Shampoo (regular and dry)
- [ ] Body wipes
- [ ] Bodywash
- [ ] Flip flops (for showers)

Healthcare

- [ ] Contacts, case, and solution
- [ ] Chapstick
- [ ] Sunscreen
- [ ] Shaving cream
- [ ] Razor
- [ ] Comb/Brush
- [ ] Anti-allergy tablets
- [ ] Upset stomach medicines
- [ ] Pain relief
- [ ] Antiseptic cream
- [ ] Plasters and bandages

Bathroom Necessities

- [ ] Towel
- [ ] Brush/Comb/Sponge
- [ ] Toilet paper (biodegradable)
- [ ] Cassette toilet & chemicals
- [ ] Bucket/Bivvy loo
- [ ] Rubbish bag

Clothes/Outerwear

- [ ] Underwear
- [ ] Socks
- [ ] Long/short sleeve shirts
- [ ] Long/short trousers

- [ ] Waterproof clothes
- [ ] Sweatshirt/Hoodie
- [ ] Pyjamas
- [ ] Hat (sunhat or woolly)
- [ ] Walking boots
- [ ] Spare/smart shoes
- [ ] Swimwear

Essential Camp Kit

- [ ] Window blinds
- [ ] Tailgate lock
- [ ] Anti-condensation granules
- [ ] Door mat for muddy shoes
- [ ] Awning/tent, poles, and pegs
- [ ] Mallet
- [ ] Tarpaulin/Groundsheet
- [ ] Paracord
- [ ] Fold-out roof awning
- [ ] Hammock
- [ ] Lighter/matches
- [ ] Swiss Army knife
- [ ] Pop-up toilet/storage tent
- [ ] Water storage (collapsible)
- [ ] Rechargeable cooling fan
- [ ] Tent sealer/repair kit
- [ ] Microfibre towels
- [ ] Rooftop cargo bag
- [ ] Solar panel and leads
- [ ] Solar/USB shower
- [ ] Hot water bottle
- [ ] Barbeque

Sleep gear

- [ ] Pillow or other padding
- [ ] Sleeping bag/duvet
- [ ] Sleeping mat
- [ ] Extra blanket
- [ ] Pet bed
- [ ] Cot

Drinks

- [ ] Coffee/Tea/Sugar
- [ ] Hot chocolate mix
- [ ] Powdered milk
- [ ] Cold drinks

Dinnerware

- ☐ Folding table and chairs
- ☐ Bowls
- ☐ Plates
- ☐ Mugs
- ☐ Cutlery
- ☐ Drinking glasses

Cookware

- ☐ Stove and spare fuel
- ☐ Fuel hoses and adapters
- ☐ Kettle
- ☐ Pans
- ☐ Cutting block and knife
- ☐ Serving spoon
- ☐ Tongs
- ☐ Can opener
- ☐ Aluminium foil
- ☐ Ziplock bags
- ☐ Paper towels
- ☐ Washing up liquid
- ☐ Collapsible washing up bowl
- ☐ Insulated bag for picnics/takeaways

Repairs

- ☐ Duct tape
- ☐ Cable ties

Cleaning

- ☐ Dust pan & brush
- ☐ Old towel
- ☐ Something to mop up spills
- ☐ Bag for wet/muddy gear

Hobbies

- ☐ Use your own list for these prompts
- ☐ Hiking
- ☐ Running
- ☐ Swimming
- ☐ Kayaking
- ☐ Cycling
- ☐ Photography
- ☐ Videography
- ☐ Bluetooth speaker
- ☐ Fishing
- ☐ Late night walks
- ☐ Musical instrument
- ☐ Puzzles and games
- ☐ Reading
- ☐ Downloaded TV/Films
- ☐ Writing
- ☐ Drawing
- ☐ Painting
- ☐ Crafts
- ☐ Plant ID book
- ☐ Wildlife ID book
- ☐ Binoculars (bird watching)
- ☐ Pens/pencils
- ☐ Notebook

Important Things to Bring

Jot down some notes of what you want to take with you on the Fosse Way.

Apps

Travelling by Car

Google Maps
Add 'near me' to your search to find local matches for your searches, for example 'chip shops near me'. You can download an area beforehand.

Waze
Good for live-traffic up updates.

PetrolPrices
Find the nearest, cheapest fuel.

What3words
Great for finding rural places. More accurate than using the postcode.

Circuit
Used by delivery drivers to find the most efficient route between waypoints. Great for planning a stage to take in the places you want to see.

Public Transport

Google Maps
Great for planning buses or trains if you fancy a break from driving.

UK Bus Checker
Excellent tool for telling you when a bus is due at your stop.

Train Track
Another great tool for telling you when a train is due and which platform.

Walking

OS Maps
Good for exploring green spaces.

Komoot and Go Jauntly
Suggestions for recreational biking and walking routes.

E-Walk
Excellent for finding shortcuts and green spaces in urban locations.

Where is Public Toilet
Handy for finding places in shopping centres, cafes and shops.

Cycling

CycleStreets and **BikeMap**
Route planning services for cyclists with settings for mountain and road bikes.

History

National Trust, English Heritage, Historic Houses Association
Lists the details of their properties such as prices, opening times, parking, and facilities.

Entertainment

Remember to download what you want to watch before you go away to save your data.

- Alexa (read Kindle books aloud)
- Kindle
- Netflix
- Amazon Prime
- SkyGo
- TV channel players
- Podcasts
- Ticket booking
- Viator
- Ticketmaster
- Skiddle
- Eventbrite
- Bandsintown
- Duolingo (for learning Latin)

Camping

Camping membership apps
For the clubs you are a member of.

Searchforsites
Find places to stop when out and about and for places to park up overnight.

Archies
A large database of UK campsites.

Packpoint
Handy packing list app so you can make sure nothing important gets left behind. Add your own custom lists to the suggested essentials.

Key Websites

Tourism

These sites are handy for checking for further details before you visit.

- www.nationaltrust.org.uk
- www.english-heritage.org.uk
- www.visitengland.com
- www.visitdevon.com
- www.visitsomerset.co.uk
- www.cotswolds.info
- visit.warwickshire.gov.uk
- www.visitleicester.info
- www.visit-nottinghamshire.co.uk
- www.visitlincolnshire.com

Camping

Online site directories

- www.coolcamping.com
- www.pitchup.com
- www.campsites.co.uk
- www.ukcampsite.co.uk/sites
- campingandcaravanningclub.co.uk
- www.caravanclub.co.uk

HANDY TIPS FOR MICROCAMPING

Take extra fuel for cooking

The most common type of stove uses butane or propane gas canisters. Make sure you have ample supplies. You might get through more than you think, especially on cold or windy days, and not every campsite has a shop.

Take an insulated picnic bag

Great for bringing takeaways home hot, else for bringing frozen food and water bottles from home so it keeps cold for a bit longer out of the fridge. Remember too that the fuller your bag is, the better it will maintain its temperature.

Have a cooking essentials box

It's easy to forget things like spatulas, scissors and bottle or can openers, so pack a kitchen utensils box to take with you. Look out for multi-tool utensils like large 'sporks' that can flip, drain, serve or stir food.

Take something to light your stove or BBQ

If you are staying at a campsite that allows barbecues make sure you take something to light it with. Also, a handy backup to your cooker ignition system.

Plan meals in advance

This helps you bring the right long-life foods with you to make a meal in an emergency, and it helps makes sure you have the right utensils and pans for your meals.

Use spray oil for cooking

A small amount of spray oil in a travel bottle is much more convenient for cooking than taking a huge bottle from home.

Take a folding water carrier

A collapsible water carrier that easily dispenses water is a camping must-have. Pans and people need a rinse every now and again. A collapsible carrier wastes less space as you use the water.

Collect condiment sachets

Amazon and eBay and bargain home stores sell lots of foodstuffs in sachets. Sometimes, you might be given some extras at a fast food joint—salt, pepper, sauces, jams etc. The handy miniature sizes make them ideal for cooking on the road.

Take a hot water bottle

A hot water bottle is a great way to keep warm in your car or van. Even the best quality sleeping bag will benefit from the extra heat generated, helping you sleep well instead of lying awake shivering all night.

Take a lantern

Whilst torches have their place, if you want to relax, a lantern will provide a more practical and soothing light source. If you forget to bring one, point your torch at a filled water bottle and it will diffuse the light.

Fairy lights as night lights

Battery powered fairy lights produce a lovely gentle glow and look pretty. Pick a set with a remote control so it's easy to switch them on and off when you're in bed. If you're careful, you can twizzle spiral upholstery pins into your roof fabric, or use magnets with hooks to pin them up. Alternatively, see if you can push the metal handle of small bulldog clips in between the upholstery or headliner fabric to hold up the wire.

Make sure you know how to pitch your awning before you get to the campsite

On a relaxed sunny afternoon pitching a new awning isn't such a headache, but imagine getting stuck in traffic, arriving late and then the heavens opening. It also gives you an opportunity to pay attention to how your awning is packed so you stand a fighting chance of getting it back in the bag the same way. Take some photos as you unpack it the first time. If you forget, don't worry, there are usually manufacturers' videos on YouTube that explain more.

Unzip windows and doors to put your awning away

You're less likely to trap air in the fabric and it will fold up smaller.

Bring a pair of slip on shoes

These are handy to put on if you need to pop outside quickly.

Take a waterproof door mat to stand on

In wet weather your camper can quickly get muddy. Having a doormat acts like a bit of a barrier helping to keep the inside of your car dry and clean. Have a bin bag handy to store muddy footwear.

Keep a camping essentials box always packed

Put together your own camping essentials box and include things like duct tape, a multi-tool, first aid kit, torch, matches and so on. That way, you'll know you've always got those random things that you always seem to need.

Use jumbo shopping bags for packing

These make packing a doddle. They are large enough to fit sleeping bags and pillows inside, and transporting in bags like this means if you are setting up or taking down in the rain, your camping gear won't get wet. Use different colours for different things, it helps keep things organised.

Take something to charge your essential devices

A USB battery pack is ideal for charging up your phone if you're using it for navigating or entertainment. Look for one over 10,000 mAh to do multiple charges. You can use a 240v inverter with a 3-pin plug socket to charge up low-power devices like laptops as you drive.

Take cleaning wipes for spills

Kitchen roll and microfibre tea towels are great for dealing with mishaps.

Pack extra layers

Regardless of the time of year, dressing in layers is a good idea when it comes to spending time outdoors. Make sure you've got plenty of warm layers, waterproofs and so on.

Pay attention to how you pack your car

When you pack the car, make sure the things you will need first are easily accessible. That means you won't have to unpack everything before you can get to them—especially handy if you end up having to set up in the rain.

Bring the right sleeping bag

Sleeping bags, like your duvet at home, have a tog rating that tells you how well insulated it is and how warm it is likely to keep you. A cheap one-season sleeping bag is very light and unlikely to keep you toasty unless its summer. Look for a three- or four-season bag to ensure you'll be comfortable in the colder months. A bag with an integral hood is great for winter too. Else bring a woolly hat just in case you need it.

Don't go to bed cold

If you're prone to cold feet, if you get into your sleeping bag cold, you are likely to stay chilly. Before you go to bed, have a warm drink, or go for a brisk walk to the toilet block to warm up your core temperature a little before settling down for the night.

Use a sleeping bag liner

Consider buying a bag liner. These are said to add an extra 'season' of warmth. They come in silk or flannel material and are an easy way to adjust the temperature of your bag when you're on the road.

Invest in some heat packs

Heat packs are useful. Popping a couple in your pockets can make a real difference. There are chemical ones that are single or multi use, or you can get rechargeable USB electric ones.

Quick Tips

- Use strong 'neodymium' magnets to connect awnings to cars and hang things up.

- A mosquito net can cover your tailgate to stop midges coming in. Handy for those Scotland trips...

- A hanging shoe rack, or back-of-seat organiser is handy for keeping frequently used items close to hand and out of the way.

- Bring some loose change for parking meters and small purchases like coffees or snacks.

- 7-day pill boxes with the flip-top lids are good for storing a selection of herbs, just relabel the lids with the name of the herb or spice rather than the day.

- Sachet drinks of hot chocolate, or coffee with milk and sugar are handy for hot drinks as they don't need chilled milk.

- If you have a gym membership with a large chain, you've got access to a shower.

- A 12-volt car kettle is good for hot drinks, as well as cuppa soups and pot noodles. It takes around 15 minutes to boil the water and needs the car engine running, so you can only use it when you're travelling, but with a bit of planning, it's a great alternative to getting the gas cooker out when you arrive somewhere.

- A microfibre towel is good for dealing with window condensation. Cut down on the amount that forms by putting condensation gel bags under the seats, and insulating your windows with blackout blinds.

- Car window wind deflectors and tailgate locks are good for leaving the windows and tailgate open a little a night.

- Scope out coffee shops in the area if you need good WiFi and mains power. Get loyalty apps for food and drink shops to help find them and check what facilities they have.

- Take a portable jump start in case you get stranded somewhere. Some of them also double up as backup power for your phone or tablet.

- Check your owner's manual to make sure you know how to turn the alarm and any interior lights off. Practice before you go away.

- Build a wooden sleeping platform so you can store things underneath your bed/seating area. Look up 'boot jumps' on the internet for ideas. You can also make your own simple set up with heavy-duty plastic storage boxes with an inflatable mattress on the top. Check Facebook groups and YouTube for lots more tips from other campers.

- Use a 12-volt bento box (like a heated lunch box) to heat canned meals as you drive. Hot dogs are nice and easy to reheat quickly. So are crumpets with butter. Remember you'll need to keep the engine running to use your bento box, so switch it on in good time as you travel so you can eat when you arrive.

- Get the most out of google maps by searching for 'XYZ near me' and 'XYZ along the route', for example 'petrol stations along the route'.

- Consider getting a cheap tablet for doing research on the road, it's less fiddly that fighting with a tiny phone screen—and it's good for watching films too. You can 'tether' your tablet to your mobile phone so you can share the internet connection.

- If you need to do a lot of typing when you're away, invest in a bluetooth keyboard and mouse to go with your tablet to save taking a bulky or expensive laptop with you.

ROAD TRIP GAMES

Spotting Things

Allocate some points for spotting things as you drive along:

- A private number plate
- A field of cows or sheep
- A yellow vehicle
- A specific road sign, for example 'no right turn'

Word Games

The List Game

- Pick a category and take it in turns to add an item to the list, for example 'places ending in -cester, -caster or -ceister'. They are usually on the site of former Roman settlements.

The Rhyme Game

- Pick a word then take it in turns to say things that rhyme with it.

ROMAN MOVIES

Here's a list of 'sword and sandal' classics, chosen by Dr Gregory Aldrete, Professor of History at the University of Wisconsin. Something to watch on a night in.

Quo Vadis

The movie that kickstarted the sword and sandal genre

Few films have had as much influence on modern filmgoers' perceptions of ancient Rome as 'Quo Vadis'. MGM Studios' 1951 release of this film, with its irresistible formula of evil, arrogant Romans versus virtuous, devout Christians, ushered in the golden age of this type of picture.

Ben-Hur

The greatest chariot race

'Ben-Hur', released in 1959, was a huge financial risk that turned out to be a money machine for MGM Studios.

Spartacus

Kubrick's controversial epic

'Spartacus', despite being one of the most well-known ancient Rome film epics, is a bit of an outlier. It's a gladiator film with only one fight scene.

Cleopatra

A wild spectacle

'Cleopatra', released in 1963, brought about the demise of the golden age of epic films set in ancient Rome. During production, the film gained notoriety for its massive cost overruns and production issues, which included changes in director and cast, a change in filming location, sets that had to be built twice, and personal scandal surrounding co-stars Taylor and Burton. It was the most expensive film ever made up to that point, nearly bankrupting 20th Century Fox.

The Fall of the Roman Empire

The expensive flop

'The Fall of the Roman Empire' was a complete financial disaster, costing $19 million and earning $4.75 million.

The title of the film refers to the onset of corruption and decadence that led to Rome's demise, rather than the final fall of the Roman empire, which did, in fact, survive for centuries after the period depicted in the film. It delves deeply into the issue of imperial succession, examining both the father-son relationship against the backdrop of imperial politics, as well as the nature and limits of loyalty and friendship.

I, Claudius

The BBC makes an Anti-Epic

The 1976, BBC production of 'I, Claudius' with veteran thespian Derek Jacobi in the title role, has been hailed as one of the most influential and memorable portraits of the ancient world ever to be seen on the big or small screen. The miniseries, set between 24 BC and 54 AD, provided an intimate look at the reigns of emperors Augustus, Tiberius, Caligula, and Claudius.

The Life Of Brian

Parodying conventions

Monty Python's 'Life of Brian', is a witty parody of both biblical and Roman epic films, which tackles gladiatorial games, ancient Roman society and religion, and the human proclivity for factionalism and tribalism.

Gladiator

The resurrected historical epic

The 2000 film 'Gladiator' resurrected a genre that had been dormant for nearly 40 years. It was inspired by Daniel P. Mannix's 1958 book 'Those About to Die' (formerly titled 'The Way of the Gladiator').

Rome

HBO's look at Ancient History

The HBO miniseries 'Rome' is the best place to look to get a sense of what life was like for the average person in ancient Rome. This short-lived series provided accurate (if gritty) perspectives on ancient Roman society.

The Centurion and The Eagle

Legions in the United Kingdom

These two films are based on the legendary story of an ancient Roman legion lost in the mists of Britain, the Roman Empire's Ninth Legion who vanished in Caledonia in the early second century. 'Centurion' and 'The Eagle' provide solid insights into Roman military tactics.

ROMAN TRAVEL

A Roman carpentum carriage. Carole Raddato Wiki Commons

Vehicle Options

The ancient Romans relied on several modes of transportation, the most basic of which was travelling on foot! Carriages were mainly used to move goods or cover long distances. They made a racket as they moved with their iron-shod wheels. There was no rubber back then. In major cities such as Rome, carriages were prohibited during the day, so residents had to put up with the rumbling of their wheels at night.

The *plaustrum* was a popular. Primarily, it was used to transport construction materials and agricultural products such as cereals, olive oil, and wine. It performed a similar role to a modern pick-up truck. It was made of a wooden board with two to four thick wheels. Adding a top or sides

was uncommon. The plaustrum was drawn by two muscular oxen.

The *essedum* was a two-wheeled chariot with no top and a closed front that could accommodate two standing passengers. When one or more horses or mules were used to pull it, it moved quickly.

The *cisium* was more sluggish. It had two wheels, no roof, a seat for two passengers, and one or two mules or horses pulled it. It was either driven by a 'taxi driver' or by the passenger themselves.

The *raeda* was the forerunner of today's buses. It had four wheels, several benches, and storage space for luggage. Like travelling by air these days, there was a weight limit for baggage. There was either no top or a simple cloth put on. It was pulled by many oxen, mules, or horses for up to four hours at a time!

Wealthy Travellers

Affluent Romans, especially the women, would use a 'litter' to travel around the city or on very short trips. One or two seated people would be transported by six slaves (bearers). It meant they could avoid contact with working-class Romans. The city streets were not always safe, especially for beautiful rich women.

The *carpentum* was the 'limousine' for the wealthy. It was built more like a camper with four wheels, a wooden arched roof, and a comfortable, spacious, and tastefully decorated interior.

The *carruca* looked like a tiny carpentum. It had two seats and was primarily used by the wealthy Romans. To make the ride more comfortable, both the carpentum and carruca had suspension as well as metal and leather straps.

Roman Road Trips

Traveling during the time of the Romans was slow and exhausting. Journeying from Rome to Naples took six days, according to ORBIS, Stanford University's 'Google Maps' routing tool for the Ancient World, compared to about two hours and twenty minutes today.

Because most carriages lacked suspension and had metal wheels, they were extremely uncomfortable to ride in, making travel even on the paved Roman roads uncomfortable, exhausting, and noisy.

Plan an ancient route here:

- orbis.stanford.edu

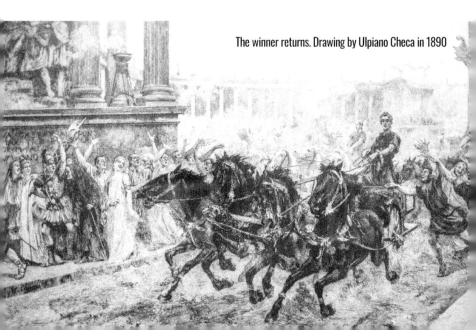

The winner returns. Drawing by Ulpiano Checa in 1890

ROME'S ROAD NETWORK

Roman road in Pompeii

The Impact of Roman Roads

The empire had an extensive system that stretched from northern England to southern Egypt, reaching a total of 74,500 miles at its peak.

For their time, Roman roads were advanced and reliable. Even during the Middle Ages, no better roads had been constructed. Hundreds of years after the fall of the Roman Empire, many are still in use.

How the roads were built

The Romans would first lay the kerb stones, then dig a long pit along a specific trajectory determined by a surveyor. The pit would be filled with a compacted layer of rock, sand, or gravel. Then another layer of finer gravel would be added.

A layer of concrete would be poured over this foundation, and the road would be paved with large slabs of rock. To make the road surface smoother, a thinner layer of concrete would be applied. On the surviving original roads, that surface layer has worn out, leaving the cobbled slabs beneath.

Thanks to this construction method, the roads could withstand freezing and flooding. Most importantly, they would last a very long time with little maintenance.

The Twelve Tables tablets, where Rome's early laws were described, stated that straight sections of roads should be 8 feet wide. Bends were to be 16 feet wide.

Major roads, ran in a straight line and connected two cities that were often hundreds of miles apart. Other important cities along their path could only be reached via branch roads.

Because of the scale of these unwavering roads, massive land excavation and the transport of materials over long distances was required, bridges, tunnels, and viaducts had to be built wherever roads encountered major geographical obstacles. This required colossal engineering feats.

Toll booths and rest stops

Today, roads and infrastructure are built primarily for economic reasons, in order to facilitate the movement of goods and people. During the Roman era, roads were primarily constructed for military purposes, allowing legions to move quickly and consolidate newly conquered lands.

Nonetheless, roads played an important economic role by facilitating the movement of resources. Major thoroughfares had tolls, just like some of our roads today. They were frequently found at bridges or city gates.

Couriers used major roads to transport written communications. Unlike today, carrying mail was a dangerous job, with couriers frequently becoming the target of criminal gangs.

The government built *mansiones*, 'staying places', at regular intervals, which were typically 16 to 19 miles apart. These rest stops provided refreshments and accommodation and were similar to what we have today. However, they had a bad reputation for being frequented by prostitutes and thieves.

Businesses grew up around these areas, and sometimes small towns sprung up too. There would occasionally be a military camp nearby, as well as villas set up specifically for officials.

PLACES TO EAT

Exeter, Devon

The Cork and Tile Portuguese
££ - £££   Mediterranean, Vegetarian Friendly   15 Gandy Street, Exeter EX4 3LS

Harry's Restaurant
££ - £££   British, Vegetarian, Vegan Friendly   86 Longbrook Street, Exeter EX4 6AP

Red Panda
£   Fast food, Asian Healthy   29 Gandy Street, Exeter EX4 3LS

Taco-Macho Food
£   Mexican, Fast food, Vegetarian Friendly   122 Fore Street, Exeter EX4 3JQ

Opa Bar Restaurant
££ - £££   Bar, Mediterranean, Greek   36-37 South Street, Exeter EX1 1ED

The Fat Pig Exeter
££ - £££   British, Pub, Vegetarian Friendly   2 John Street, Exeter EX1 1BL

Dinosaur Café
£   Café, Mediterranean, European   New North Road, Exeter EX4 4HH

Honiton, Devon

Sawatdee
££ - £££   Asian. Thai   166 High Street, Honiton EX14 1JX

Ali's Kebab House
£   Fast food, Turkish   135A High Street, Honiton EX14 1HR

The Holt
££ - £££   Bar, European, British   178 High Street, Honiton EX14 1LA

The Yellow Deli
££ - £££   Café, International, British   43-47 High Street, Honiton EX14 1PW

Axminster, Devon

River Cottage Kitchen

| ££ - £££ | British, Healthy, Vegetarian Friendly | Trinity Square, Axminster EX13 5AN |

Axminster Inn

| ££ - £££ | Bar, British, Pub | Silver Street, Axminster EX13 5AH |

Arts Cafe Bar

| £ | Café, British, Vegetarian Friendly | Church St, Old Courthouse, Axminster EX13 5AQ |

Ilchester, Somerset

Nuova Italia Restaurant

| ££ - £££ | Italian, Pizza, European | 18 Church Street, Ilchester, Yeovil BA22 8LN |

The Ilchester Arms Restaurant

| ££ - £££ | Bar, British, Pub | The Square Ilchester, Yeovil BA22 8LH |

Claire's Of Ilchester

| £ | Café, British, Vegetarian Friendly | Church Street, Ilchester, Yeovil BA22 8LW |

Ponto de Encontro

| ££ | Portuguese | 6 Town Street, Shepton Mallet BA4 5BG |

Collett Park Café

| £ | Café British | Park Road, Shepton Mallet BA4 5BP |

Radstock, Somerset

Castello Restaurant

| ££ - £££ | Italian, Pizza, Mediterranean | 5 The Street, Radstock BA3 3PZ |

The Riverbank

| ££ - £££ | Café, British, Greek | 1 Frome Rd County Br, Radstock BA3 3AB |

Bath, Somerset, UK

Menu Gordon Jones

| ££££ | European British Vegetarian Friendly | 2 Wellsway, Bath BA2 3AQ |

Eight

| ££ - £££ | European British Contemporary | 3 North Parade Passage, Bath BA1 1NX |

Jc's kitchen

| £ | Philippine Fast food Barbecue | Bog Island, Terrace Walk, Bath BA1 1LN |

LJ Hugs

| £ | Cajun & Creole, Fast food, Vegetarian Friendly | Southgate Street, Bath BA1 1AQ |

1. The Salamander

| ££-£££ | British pub | 3 John Street, Bath BA1 2JL |

Juno Bar & Kitchen

| £ | Bar Pizza Pub | Philip St Southgate Shopping Ctr, Bath BA1 1AU |

Colonna and Smalls Speciality Coffee

| ££-£££ | Coffee, Quick bites. | 6 Chapel Row, Bath BA1 1HN |

Kekolo Coffee

| ££-£££ | Quick Bites Café British | 3 New Bond Street Buildings, Bath BA1 1BL |

Castle Combe, Wiltshire

The Little Picnic Shop in Castle Combe

| ££ - £££ | British, Vegetarian, Vegan Friendly | Main Street, Castle Combe SN14 7HU |

Castle Inn Restaurant

| ££ - £££ | Bar, British, Pub | West St, Castle Combe, Chippenham SN14 7HN |

The Old Stables Coffee Shop Castle Combe

| £ | Quick Bites, Café, British | Estate Yard, Castle Combe SN14 7HO |

Malmesbury, Wiltshire

The Birdcage
££ - £££   Italian, Vegetarian Friendly   2 High Street Malmesbury Wiltshire, SN16 9AU

Whole Hog
££ - £££   Bar, British, Pub   8 Market Cross, Malmesbury SN16 9AS

The Abbey Café
££ - £££   Quick Bites, Café, British   Malmesbury Abbey, Malmesbury SN16 9FS

Cirencester, Gloucestershire

Tierra & Mar Restaurant
££ - £££   Mediterranean, European, Spanish   29 Sheep Street, Cirencester GL7 1QW

Igloo Restaurants
££ - £££   International, British, Vegetarian Friendly   37 Castle Street, Cirencester GL7 1QD

The Friar Tuck
£   Seafood, Fast food, British   64 Dyer Street, Cirencester GL7 2PF

Porters Cafe Bar
££ - £££   Fast food, Brew Pub, Cafe, British, Pub, Bar   34 Castle Street, Cirencester GL7 1QH

Toro Lounge
££ - £££   Quick Bites, Bar, Vegetarian Friendly   34 Cricklade Street, Cirencester GL7 1JH

The Twelve Bells Pub and Restaurant
££ - £££   Bar, British, Pub   12 Lewis Lane, Cirencester GL7 1EA

The Old Cafe Cirencester
££ - £££   Café, Vegetarian Friendly   50 Cricklade Street Next door to Everlasting Impressions Piercing Studio, Cirencester GL7 1JN

Lucia's
££ - £££   Café, Vegetarian Friendly   36 Dyer Street, Cirencester GL7 2PF

Bourton on the water, Gloucestershire

De la Haye's

££ - £££   British, Vegetarian   High Street, Bourton-on-the-Water GL54 2AN
           Friendly, Gluten Free

The Mousetrap Inn Restaurant

££ - £££   Bar, British, Pub   Lansdowne The Mousetrap Inn, Bourton-on-the-Water GL54 2AR

The Cornish Bakery

£   Café, Bakeries, British   15 High Street, Bourton-on-the-Water GL54 2AQ

Stow on the Wold, Gloucestershire

Le Patissier Anglais

££ - £££   French, European,   The Square, Stow-on-the-Wold GL54 1AB
           Vegetarian Friendly

Cotswold Baguettes

£   Fast food, British, Healthy   Cotswold House Church Street, Stow-on-the-Wold GL54 1BB

The Stow Lodge Hotel

££ - £££   Bar, British, Vegetarian   Market Square, Stow-on-the-Wold
           Friendly

Lucy's Tearoom and B&B

££ - £££   Café, Vegetarian Friendly   The Square, Stow-on-the-Wold GL54 1AB

Moreton in Marsh, Gloucestershire

The Spice Room

££ - £££   Indian, Asian, Balti   3 Oxford Street, Moreton-in-Marsh GL56 0LA

The Black Bear

££ - £££   Bar, British, Pub   49 High Street, Moreton-in-Marsh GL56 0AX

The Cotswold Tearoom

££ - £££   Café, British, Healthy   4 High Street, Moreton-in-Marsh GL56 0AH

Leicester, Leicestershire

Bodega Cantina
££ - £££   Mexican   6 St Martins Square, Leicester LE1 5DF

Crafty Burger
££ - £££   American, Vegetarian   Saint Martin's Square, Leicester LE1 5DG
                Friendly

Gelato Village
£   Street Food, Italian, Cafe   2 St. Martins Square, Leicester LE1 5DF

The Globe
££ - £££   Bar, British, Pub   43 Silver Street, Leicester LE1 5EU

Knight & Garter
££ - £££   Bar, British, Pub   14 Hotel Street, Leicester LE1 5AW

St Martin's Coffee Shop
££ - £££   Quick Bites, Café, British   2-6 St. Martins Walk, Leicester LE1 5DG

Hollys Coffee Shop & Sandwich Bar
£   Quick Bites, Café, British   13-15 St. Martins City Centre, Leicester LE1 5DE

Newark-upon-Trent, Nottinghamshire

Taylor's Fine Dining
££££   European, British,   25 Castle Gate, Newark-on-Trent NG24 1AZ
                Vegetarian Friendly

Koinonia Restaurant
££ - £££   Indian, Asian, Vegetarian   19 St. Marks Lane Near to NCP Car Park, Asda,
                Friendly   Newark-on-Trent NG24 1XS

Dinner Jackets
£   Café, Fast food   8 Lombard Street, Newark-on-Trent NG24 1XB

Madisons
££ - £££   British, Pub, Gastropub   37 Carter Gate, Newark-on-Trent NG24 1UA

The Flying Circus
££ - £££   Bar, Pub   53 Castle Gate, Newark-on-Trent NG24 1BE

Newark-upon-Trent, Nottinghamshire (Continued)

Pastability Newark
££ - £££   Italian, Café,   17 Carter Gate, Newark-on-Trent NG24 1UA
               Mediterranean

Gannets Daycafé
££ - £££   Quick Bites, Café, European   35 Castle Gate, Newark-on-Trent NG24 1AZ

Lincoln, Lincolnshire

Kine
££ - £££   European, British,   6 West Parade, Lincoln LN1 1JT
               Vegetarian Friendly

Lawson's bar & bistro
££ - £££   Italian, French, British   8-9 The Strait, Lincoln LN2 1JD

Cafe Shanti
£   Street Food, Café, Healthy   6 Clasketgate, Lincoln LN2 1JS

Chef Phong Thai Takeaway
£   Fast food, Asian, Thai   11 Corporation Street, Lincoln LN2 1HL

The Dandy Lion
££ - £££   Bar, Pub   3 Newland, Lincoln LN1 1UX

The Mailbox
££ - £££   Quick Bites, Bar, British   19-20 Guildhall Street, Lincoln LN1 1TR

Margaret's Tea Rooms
££ - £££   Café, British, Healthy   13B Garmston Street, Lincoln LN2 1HZ

Lady Rose's Edwardian Tea Room
££ - £££   Café, Vegetarian Friendly   Free School Lane Unit 1, Lincoln LN2 1EY

CAMPSITES

Campsites all have their own distinct personalities—some are vast and sprawling with things like discos, children's play areas, cafes, shops and even swimming pools. Others have a much wilder, back-to-basics vibe, so be mindful of the kind of camping experience you want and make sure you choose your campsite accordingly. Once you've chosen a campsite, before you arrive, make sure you are aware of the campsite's rules. These can range from absolutely no noise after 9pm to no music, dogs or campfires, so make sure you are aware of the rules and that you stick to them. Make sure you know check in and check out times and print out some details, just in case your phone goes flat.

Devon

Barley Meadow Touring Park
Crockernwell, Exeter, Devon, England, EX6 6NR

Postwood Gardens Campsite
Kentisbeare, Cullompton, Devon, England, EX15 2BS

Hunters Lodge Inn
Charmouth Road, Axminster, Devon (South), EX13 5SZ

South Somerset Holiday Park
Turnpike, A30 Exeter Road, Chard, Somerset, TA20 3EA

Castle Brake Holiday Park
Castle Lane, Woodbury, Exeter, Devon, England, EX5 1HA

West Down Orchard Touring and Camping Park
Lopen Head, South Petherton, Somerset, England, TA13 5JH

Bovey's Down Farm
Farway, Colyton, Honiton, Devon, England, EX24 6JD

Somerset

The Masons Arms
41 Lower Odcombe, Odcombe, Yeovil, Somerset, England, BA22 8TX

The Cross Keys Inn
Lydford-on-Fosse, Somerton, Somerset, England, TA11 7HA

The Brook House Inn & Touring Park
Station Road, Castle Cary, Somerset, BA7 7PF

Somerset (continued)

Glastonbury Camping and Caravanning
Higher Edgarley House, Glastonbury, Somerset, England, BA6 8LB

Tucker's Grave Inn and Campsite
Knoll Lane, Faulkland, Bath, Somerset, England, BA3 5XF

Farleigh Road Camping
Farleigh Road, Norton St Philip, Somerset, Eng-land, BA2 7NG

Boyd Valley Lake
Golden Valley Lane, Bitton, Bristol, Greater Bristol, England, BS30 6NY

Gloucestershire

The Thames Head Inn
Tetbury Road, Cirencester, Gloucestershire, Eng-land, GL7 6NZ

The New Inn Willersey
The New Inn Willersey,

Mayfield Park , Main Street, Willersey, Gloucestershire, WR12 7PJ

Stow-on-the-Wold Rugby Club
Oddington Road, Stow-on-the-Wold, Cheltenham, Gloucestershire, England, GL54 1JJ

Oxfordshire

Wysdom Touring Park
Burford School, Rear Entrance To School, Off The A361, Burford, Oxfordshire, OX18 4JG

The Old Dairy Farm Caravan and Camping
School Lane, Cropredy, Banbury, Oxfordshire, Eng-land, OX17 1PX

Warwickshire

Cotswolds Camping
Holycombe, Whichford, Shipston On Stour, War-wickshire, England, CV36 5PH

Eriba Glade Touring Caravan And Camping Site
Peacehaven, Frankton Lane, Stretton On Dun-smore, Rugby, Warwickshire, CV23 9JQ

Warwickshire (continued)

Wigrams,
Wigrams, Tomlow Road, Napton-on-the-Hill, Southam, Warwickshire, CV47 8HX

Dodwell Park
Evesham Road, Stratford-upon-Avon, Warwick-shire, England, CV37 9SR

Green Gates Caravan Park
Green Gates, Kings Lane, Stratford-upon-Avon, Warwickshire, England, CV37 0QA

Makins Lakes
Makins Fisheries, Bazzard Road, Bramcote, War-wickshire, England, CV11 6QJ

Leicestershire

Sysonby Acres Leisure Park,
Asfordby Road, Melton Mow-bray, Leicestershire, LE13 0HW

Holly Farm Fishery Moby Park
Willoughby Road, Ashby Magna, Leicestershire, LE17 5NP

Lime Tree Caravan Park
Limes Farm, Main Road, Ratcliffe Culey, Leicestershire, England, CV9 3PD

Nottinghamshire

Kelham Hall and Country Park
Main Road, Kelham, Newark, Nottinghamshire, NG23 5QX

Lincolnshire

Oakhill Leisure
Swinderby Road, Norton Disney, Lincoln, Lincolnshire, England, LN6 9QG

Forest View Camping
Hoop Lane, Apley, Market Rasen, Lincolnshire, England, LN8 5JR

Bainside House
Roughton Road, Kirkby-on-Bain, Woodhall Spa, Lincolnshire, LN10 6YL

Rectory Farm
Beckingham, Lincoln, Lincolnshire, England, LN5 0RD

INDEX

COPYRIGHT

Maps are reproduced under licence from the Ordnance Survey.

First published in the UK in 2021.

ISBN: 9798540793810

Printed in Great Britain
by Amazon

87409751R00072